The Makeover

by

Patsy Hester Daussat

NEW YORK HOLLYWOOD LONDON TORONTO

SAMUELFRENCH.COM

The Makeover cover artwork/graphic image
by etzetera creative services, Dallas, TX

Copyright © 2008 by Patsy Hester Daussat
ALL RIGHTS RESERVED

CAUTION: Professionals and amateurs are hereby warned that *THE MAKEOVER* is subject to a royalty. It is fully protected under the copyright laws of the United States of America, the British Commonwealth, including Canada, and all other countries of the Copyright Union. All rights, including professional, amateur, motion picture, recitation, lecturing, public reading, radio broadcasting, television and the rights of translation into foreign languages are strictly reserved. In its present form the play is dedicated to the reading public only.

The amateur live stage performance rights to *THE MAKEOVER* are controlled exclusively by Samuel French, Inc., and royalty arrangements and licenses must be secured well in advance of presentation. PLEASE NOTE that amateur royalty fees are set upon application in accordance with your producing circumstances. When applying for a royalty quotation and license please give us the number of performances intended, dates of production, your seating capacity and admission fee. Royalties are payable one week before the opening performance of the play to Samuel French, Inc., at 45 W. 25th Street, New York, NY 10010.

Royalty of the required amount must be paid whether the play is presented for charity or gain and whether or not admission is charged.

Stock royalty quoted upon application to Samuel French, Inc.

For all other rights than those stipulated above, apply to: Samuel French, Inc., at 45 W. 25th Street, New York, NY 10010.

Particular emphasis is laid on the question of amateur or professional readings, permission and terms for which must be secured in writing from Samuel French, Inc.

Copying from this book in whole or in part is strictly forbidden by law, and the right of performance is not transferable.

Whenever the play is produced the following notice must appear on all programs, printing and advertising for the play: "Produced by special arrangement with Samuel French, Inc."

Due authorship credit must be given on all programs, printing and advertising for the play.

ISBN 978-0-573-66266-9   Printed in U.S.A.   #15758

No one shall commit or authorize any act or omission by which the copyright of, or the right to copyright, this play may be impaired.

No one shall make any changes in this play for the purpose of production.

Publication of this play does not imply availability for performance. Both amateurs and professionals considering a production are strongly advised in their own interests to apply to Samuel French, Inc., for written permission before starting rehearsals, advertising, or booking a theatre.

No part of this book may be reproduced, stored in a retrieval system, or transmitted in any form, by any means, now known or yet to be invented, including mechanical, electronic, photocopying, recording, videotaping, or otherwise, without the prior written permission of the publisher.

IMPORTANT BILLING AND CREDIT REQUIREMENTS

All producers of *THE MAKEOVER* must give credit to the Author of the Play in all programs distributed in connection with performances of the Play, and in all instances in which the title of the Play appears for the purposes of advertising, publicizing or otherwise exploiting the Play and/or a production. The name of the Author *must* appear on a separate line on which no other name appears, immediately following the title and *must* appear in size of type not less than fifty percent of the size of the title type.

MUSIC NOTE:

Original music for 'Facing Facts' Theme song by Marhsall Such (ASCAP) Contact for music use: 817.781.4453 marshall.such@verison.net

THE MAKEOVER was first produced April 4 - 20, 2008 at Grapevine's Runway Theatre in the Dallas-Fort Worth area. It was directed by Patsy Daussat. The assistant director was Amber Sebastian. The production featured sets by Rick Daussat, costumes by Shelley Keltner, lights by Emilie Buske, sound by Jeremy Ferman, mural by Judy Bauman Blalock, make-up by Harry Friedman. The *Facing Facts* theme song was composed by Marshall Such. Technical operators were Karen Hurtado and Amy Pennington. The stage managers were Linda Fullhart and Donna Maddamma. The cast was as follows:

MELANIE BARNSWORTH . . . . Sheila D. Rose
MIKE BARNSWORTH . . . . Andrew Burns
PAULA GIACOBI . . . . Julie Aylor
VICTOR GIACOBI . . . . Dan Duncan
KEITH BARNSWORTH . . . . Charles Carroll
RICKY GIACOBI . . . . Adam Henderson
FRANCES MONTGOMERY . . . . J. Christine Lanning
MONICA . . . . Jill Ethridge
BOZ . . . . Vince Connor
JOEY MONTEGO (Voiceover) . . . . Rick Daussat

Graphic design by Sherry Etzel, etzetera creative services, Dallas Texas.

No one shall commit or authorize any act or omission by which the copyright of, or the right to copyright, this play may be impaired.

No one shall make any changes in this play for the purpose of production.

Publication of this play does not imply availability for performance. Both amateurs and professionals considering a production are strongly advised in their own interests to apply to Samuel French, Inc., for written permission before starting rehearsals, advertising, or booking a theatre.

No part of this book may be reproduced, stored in a retrieval system, or transmitted in any form, by any means, now known or yet to be invented, including mechanical, electronic, photocopying, recording, videotaping, or otherwise, without the prior written permission of the publisher.

IMPORTANT BILLING AND CREDIT REQUIREMENTS

All producers of *THE MAKEOVER* must give credit to the Author of the Play in all programs distributed in connection with performances of the Play, and in all instances in which the title of the Play appears for the purposes of advertising, publicizing or otherwise exploiting the Play and/or a production. The name of the Author *must* appear on a separate line on which no other name appears, immediately following the title and *must* appear in size of type not less than fifty percent of the size of the title type.

MUSIC NOTE:

Original music for 'Facing Facts' Theme song by Marhsall Such (ASCAP) Contact for music use: 817.781.4453 marshall.such@verison.net

THE MAKEOVER was first produced April 4 - 20, 2008 at Grapevine's Runway Theatre in the Dallas-Fort Worth area. It was directed by Patsy Daussat. The assistant director was Amber Sebastian. The production featured sets by Rick Daussat, costumes by Shelley Keltner, lights by Emilie Buske, sound by Jeremy Ferman, mural by Judy Bauman Blalock, make-up by Harry Friedman. The *Facing Facts* theme song was composed by Marshall Such. Technical operators were Karen Hurtado and Amy Pennington. The stage managers were Linda Fullhart and Donna Maddamma. The cast was as follows:

MELANIE BARNSWORTH	Sheila D. Rose
MIKE BARNSWORTH	Andrew Burns
PAULA GIACOBI	Julie Aylor
VICTOR GIACOBI	Dan Duncan
KEITH BARNSWORTH	Charles Carroll
RICKY GIACOBI	Adam Henderson
FRANCES MONTGOMERY	J. Christine Lanning
MONICA	Jill Ethridge
BOZ	Vince Connor
JOEY MONTEGO (Voiceover)	Rick Daussat

Graphic design by Sherry Etzel, etzetera creative services, Dallas Texas.

CHARACTERS

MELANIE BARNSWORTH. An attractive, middle-class, middle-aged, happily married woman who is at least 40 pounds overweight. She is fun-loving but has not completely come to terms with her weight issue. She loves being a domestic engineer.

MIKE BARNSWORTH. Her handsome husband, who is middle-aged, and is in good shape. He loves his wife and is understanding, but he's sometimes oblivious and doesn't always listen. He works in an office.

PAULA GIACOBI. Melanie's best friend and neighbor, who is middle-aged, thin, and attractive. She is no-nonsense but has a nurturing, comforting side. She is a domestic engineer.

VICTOR GIACOBI. Paula's husband and Mike's best friend. He is fairly attractive, middle-aged, and has a bit of a paunch. He is comical, but is sometimes overly flirtatious and can be abrasive. He owns a small construction company.

KEITH BARNSWORTH. Melanie and Mike's twenty-one year old son who is home for the summer from college. He is studying to be an architect. He's the boy-next-door type, but he is not perfect. He has a loving and caring relationship with his parents.

RICKY GIACOBI. Paula and Victor's college-aged son and Keith's best friend. He is more of a free spirit than Keith, and he's unconventional. He is studying psychology. He and his mother are very close. He cares about his father, but they are not as close.

FRANCES MONTGOMERY, The haughty, snobby, attractive, thin, flamboyant host of *Facing Facts*, which is an ambush reality television show. She has been surgically enhanced. She has a patronizing, friendly attitude on air, but is rude and selfish off air, except to Mike.

MONICA. A cute, college-aged redhead, who is Frances Montgomery's assistant. She is energetic, a bit eccentric, and very patient – she has to be, working with Frances. She will speak her mind, though.

BOZ. The cameraperson.

SETTING

Mike and Melanie Barnsworth's living room. They live in a suburb of a big city. Present day.

Act One

Scene 1: Late on a Saturday evening in June
Scene 2: The following Monday evening, 7 o'clock
Scene 3: Friday evening, almost four weeks later

Act Two

Scene 1: The following Monday evening, 7 o'clock
Scene 2: Late afternoon, the following Saturday
Scene 3: Two hours later
Scene 4: Late Sunday afternoon
Scene 5: Later that evening

"The Makeover" is dedicated to my family:
My late mother, Jeannette
Dad, John
Sister, Mary Gail
Son and daughter-in-law, Ryan and Erin
Son, Tony
And to my husband, Rick

ACT I

Scene 1

*(**SETTING:** The stylish, well-furnished living room of the Barnsworth's home, which is in a suburb of a big city. The kitchen door is DSR and the front door is US center. A big window is to the left of the door. There is an archway DSL that leads to the rest of the house, including the Barnsworth's bedroom and Keith's bedroom. The dining room table is SR center, with a matching hutch on the wall US of it. A sofa and coffee table at center, slightly DSL of the table, and a chair left of center. A rug is under the coffee table. The imaginary TV is downstage of the coffee table. If TV is real, it can be on DSL wall.)*

*(**AT RISE:** It is late on a Saturday night in June. **MELANIE**, **MIKE**, **PAULA** and **VICTOR** are playing Spades at the dining room table. Wine glasses, beer bottles and snacks are on the table. Games, including Catch Phrase, are on the hutch behind the table. **MIKE** is wearing a pastel shirt. **MELANIE** is wearing blousy clothes to hide the extra 40 to 80 pounds she carries. She is dealing cards. **MIKE** is standing, ready to go to the kitchen to get drink refills.)*

MELANIE. *(Dealing cards.)* I might as well have another one, too, Mike.

MIKE. *(Taking **MELANIE**'s glass and his empty beer bottle.)* Okay. Beer for Victor, red wine for Paula, white wine for my lovely wife. Coming right up.

PAULA. *(Rises, taking her glass and **VICTOR**'s empty bottle.)* You can't carry all that. I'll help you.

MIKE. Thanks.

9

(They exit to kitchen.)

VICTOR. No cheating, now. *(Starts sliding his foot up her leg.)* No dealing from the bottom.

MELANIE. *(Moving her leg away, laughs awkwardly.)* You're the only one who tries to get away with cheating, Victor!

VICTOR. Yeah. That's me – the getaway kid. *(Touches her again.)*

MELANIE. *(Tries to laugh it off, keeping it light.)* Yeah? So get away!

VICTOR. Ouch. I'm just being neighborly, sweet cheeks. *(Pats her cheek.)*

MELANIE. You sure you need another beer?

VICTOR. Don't be so stiff! *(Laughs at the connotation as the others enter.)* 'Bout time!

MIKE. Your beer, sir. Madame.

*(He and **PAULA** pass out the drinks.)*

MELANIE. Thanks, honey. *(Gives **MIKE** a kiss.)*

MIKE. *(Sits, looks at cards.)* So let's see what we have here. I think I'll take um, three – no four – um, three.

PAULA. Nothing like talking to the ol' partner, huh?

VICTOR. Quit your bitchin'! What's your bid?

*(**VICTOR** writes bids.)*

PAULA. The bitcher bids three – a *solid* three.

VICTOR. I'll bid five.

MELANIE. And I'll take three.

VICTOR. That's fourteen.

PAULA. The man's a genius.

VICTOR. Very funny. There's only thirteen tricks.

MIKE. Looks like someone is going down tonight.

(Men laugh.)

VICTOR. Okay, I'm high bid. Away we go… *(He leads, and they begin to play.)* That trick's mine. *(Scoops the cards up, leads.)* And how do you like this one, girls?

PAULA. Women.

VICTOR. What the hell is wrong with girls? Just play your card.

MIKE. And this one comes to Poppa. *(He leads another trick.)*

MELANIE. Paula, did you read in the paper today that they're bringing *Facing Facts* to town next Monday night? *(She wins trick, leads one.)*

PAULA. No!

MELANIE. Yes!

PAULA. Oh my god. I can't believe it! I wonder who they're going to surprise on the show?

MELANIE. More like ambush!

PAULA. Oh my god! I wonder if we know them?

VICTOR. Will you play your damn card, *woman*!

(PAULA throws down her card.)

This trick is mine! *(He scoops up cards.)* I don't see how you can stand that damn show. It's just a bunch of rigged crap.

PAULA. How profound. Victor, you astound me with your grasp of the English language.

(She and MELANIE laugh, another trick is played.)

VICTOR. Yeah? I guess I'm not high-falooting like that broad that hosts the show. *(Leads trick.)* What's her name?

MELANIE. Frances Montgomery.

VICTOR. That dame…she's had what? Six facelifts?

PAULA. She has not!

VICTOR. If they pull her any tighter, she'll be wearing nipples for earrings.

(They all laugh.)

PAULA. Victor!

VICTOR. What?

MIKE. I think it's a great show. I mean, they've helped a lot of people to…well, helped them reach goals, turn their life around…

(MELANIE *and* PAULA *stare at him.*)

MELANIE. And when have you ever watched it? You usually bolt out the door the minute we turn it on.

MIKE. Only on game nights. Just when I'm playing.

MELANIE. Oh, okay. (*To* PAULA.) Which is every Monday night.

(*She and* PAULA *giggle.*)

MIKE. Besides, isn't that what you're always saying?

MELANIE. Yeah, but –

VICTOR. It's your turn, Mike.

MIKE. What? Oh, sorry. (*He plays.*) Hah! Trump! (*He scoops up cards, leads trick.*)

PAULA. He's right, Victor. Lots of people have been helped by the show.

VICTOR. Oh, yeah? How?

MELANIE. One guy was an alcoholic – the show came to his house and helped the family with an intervention.

VICTOR. That's bullshit. No one ever got 'helped' unless they wanted to *be* helped.

MIKE. (*Takes trick.*) That's true. But maybe sometimes, when confronted publicly – on television- (*Leads another round.*) Maybe it helps people…come to Jesus – so to speak.

PAULA. Another time, they ambushed this woman who was – well, she was dog ugly, and I tell you, she was gorgeous when they got through with her. They did her nose, and everything. (*Motions toward breasts.*)

VICTOR. I should be so lucky.

PAULA. (*Notices trick, picks it up.*) Oh, I got one of my three!

MELANIE. I think we're in trouble.

PAULA. Maybe not, I have a couple up my sleeve.

VICTOR. So play already!

PAULA. Give me a minute – I'm thinking!

VICTOR. Hold the presses, she's thinking.

PAULA. Knock it off Victor! Sometimes you…

VICTOR. Sometimes I what?

MIKE. That *Facing Facts* show…sometimes they take a person and totally make them over, like Paula was saying.

(**PAULA** *leads.*)

MELANIE. That's right. Some people even get to go to a health spa for four weeks. I swear it's like heaven…lush and tropical. They fix meals that look marvelous, but are low calorie, low fat, low sodium, low cholesterol, low everything – but delicious. There's a hot tub, a sauna, a weight room…

PAULA. And the trainer – ooo, baby, I wouldn't mind pumping iron with him every day.

VICTOR. Ha! That'd be a miracle!

MIKE. That spa – pretty nice, huh?

MELANIE. It's fabulous! What a way to help you get into shape…working out in luxury is the only way to do it.

PAULA. It's the only way I'd ever do it!

MELANIE. Amen, sister!

(*They clink glasses.*)

MIKE. (*Smiles to himself.*) Amen to that!

MELANIE. Oh, this one's mine. (*She picks up trick, leads.*) We may do all right after all, girlfriend!

(*They snap fingers in 'Z' motion.*)

VICTOR. Oh for crissakes, play cards!

PAULA. Ha! Trumped your sorry butts! (*Leads card.*)

MIKE. Hey!

PAULA. Victor's sorry butt. Yours – cute butt.

VICTOR. Good thing I'm not sensitive. (*Picks up trick.*)

PAULA. You could use a little sensitivity training. Maybe we should get *you* on *Facing Facts*…four weeks of intensive therapy with…

MELANIE. With *Queer Eye for the Straight Guy*!

(*Women,* **MIKE** *laugh.*)

VICTOR. Holy crap! I'd come out of there with gelled hair, buffed nails, wearing a pastel polo shirt!

MIKE. Hey! What's wrong with that? *(He's wearing pastel.)*

VICTOR. No offense, buddy. Are we gonna play or what?

MELANIE. It's your lead!

*(All but **VICTOR** laugh.)*

VICTOR. You got me so damn flustered talking about that stupid show....

PAULA. Honestly, it's not stupid. You should watch it sometime – you might even like it.

VICTOR. Fat chance. *(Looks at **MELANIE**.)* Oh, no offense, honey. *(He starts to take trick.)*

MELANIE. None taken. *(Slaps hand over cards.)* I believe that one is mine.

VICTOR. So it is. My mistake.

*(**MELANIE** leads.)*

Ha! Perfect lead, honey. That trick is mine. And that is the game! Ha! *(He throws down last card, the rest throw their last card in; he and **MIKE** high-five.)*

MIKE. We are the kings.

VICTOR. And we beat the queens.

(They mimic the girls finger snapping.)

MIKE. We rule the roost. Cock-a-doodle-doo.

*(**MIKE** and **VICTOR** crow like roosters.)*

PAULA. You should be braying – like jackasses...

VICTOR. There sure as hell won't be any cock-a-doodling tonight.

(The men start braying.)

MELANIE. Mike, please...a little decorum – the window is open. *(Rises to pick up snacks, **MIKE** starts picking up games.)*

VICTOR. Sore losers.

PAULA. At least we beat you at Catch Phrase this time.

*(Women high-five as **MELANIE** heads to the kitchen, exits.)*

Here, let me help you. *(She helps* **MIKE** *pick up the games and cards.)*

VICTOR. You two cheat. You have that female intuition crap!

PAULA. VICTOR!

VICTOR. VICTOR! VICTOR! She's always screaming my name! Aren't you, baby? *(Slaps* **PAULA***'s bottom.)*

PAULA. Yeah, that would be me.

VICTOR. *(Crossing towards kitchen.)* I think I'll get another beer. Anyone?

MIKE. No more for me.

PAULA. I'm good.

MIKE. Oh, yeah? Come on, these go in Keith's room.

PAULA. Uh-oh, Keith's bedroom!

(They laugh, **MIKE** *exits.)*

VICTOR. *(To* **MIKE** *and* **PAULA.***)* Hey!

PAULA. Hey! *(Exits.)*

VICTOR. *(To* **MELANIE** *as she enters, goes to table to clear glasses.)* Hey, hey!

(He steps behind **MELANIE,** *putting his hands on her shoulders. She is trapped between chairs.)*

Hey there, gorgeous. Great dinner tonight. *(Rubs her shoulders.)*

MELANIE. Thanks. *(She's pressed against the table, and can't move.)*

VICTOR. You seem tense.

MELANIE. I'm not tense.

VICTOR. How does that feel? Good, huh?

MELANIE. No! *(She 'accidentally' elbows* **VICTOR.***)*

VICTOR. Ugh! *(He steps back.)*

MELANIE. *(She moves away.)* Sorry. Almost dropped the… uh…Are you all right?

VICTOR. Yeah, fine. You should learn to relax a little.

MELANIE. Oh, I am relaxed.

VICTOR. So, how 'bout another drink – huh?

MELANIE. It's getting late.

VICTOR. Ready to hop into bed, huh? Hubba, hubba.

MELANIE. I'm tired, Victor.

VICTOR. Already? Aw, you're not upset about a little innocent flirting, are you?

MELANIE. Innocent?

VICTOR. Of course. After all, you are my best friend's wife. We wouldn't want to hurt ol' Mike, now, would we?

MELANIE. Or Paula?

VICTOR. Yeah, her, too. No foul, huh?

MELANIE. Fine. Just…

(**MIKE** *and* **PAULA** *enter, laughing.*)

MIKE. So it doesn't always go off without a hitch, huh?

MELANIE. What doesn't?

PAULA. I was telling him about the episode of *Facing Facts*, when they tried to get that girl to lose her Goth look. She fought them tooth and nail.

MELANIE. It was kind of funny.

PAULA. It was hilarious! When the hairstylist turned her around and she saw all those soft curls around her face – she grabbed the electric shaver and buzzed a two-inch stripe down the middle of her head! I thought I'd wet my pants!

MELANIE. I think you did!

(*They laugh, except* **VICTOR**.)

VICTOR. Oh, yeah, wish I'd been there for that! *(Starts laughing.)* That reminds me of the time when you were pregnant, Paula.

PAULA. *(Starts laughing.)* Don't tell them.

MIKE. Now you have to. What happened?

VICTOR. We were lying in bed and Paula was what – eight months preggers?

PAULA. Eight and a half!

VICTOR. I don't remember what was so damn funny, but we got to laughing and couldn't stop. You know...hysterical. She yells, "Stop! Stop! I'm gonna pee!" She gets outta bed and starts waddling to the bathroom. Mind you, it's maybe ten feet away, at most. She gets as far as the sink...the toilet's right there...and she just stops and pees – right on the bathroom rug.

PAULA. I couldn't hold it a step farther! I swear it was the funniest thing that ever happened to me.

(As the laughter dies down, they sigh simultaneously.)

VICTOR. Yeah, those were the days.

PAULA. Ricky was so sweet – and dependent. I can't believe he's in college. How did those years fly by so fast?

MELANIE. I don't know. It seems like yesterday Keith was just a toddler. Learning the alphabet, playing peek-a-boo... Now he's studying to be an architect and I'm studying natural remedies for menopause. Whew! We're going to get depressed if we keep this up!

PAULA. I'm already depressed.

VICTOR. Yeah? Well, if we'd had more kids, you'd still have 'em at home, wouldn't ya?

PAULA. But we don't, and they're not.

VICTOR. Not my choice.

PAULA. Don't go there, Victor.

MIKE. Okay, okay. Enough of this! So, we're empty nesters... but we got each other! Besides, the guys are home for the summer, so no more moping!

PAULA. But how much do we actually see them? They stay out until two or three almost every night. *(Incredulously.)* How do they do that?

VICTOR. Cause they sleep the whole freakin' morning away.

PAULA. And then they go to work.

MELANIE. I think I'm going to cry.

MIKE. I'd cry if Keith *wasn't* working! Speaking of which, I gotta do some office work in the morning. We better call it a night.

VICTOR. Yeah, you better get this old man home, Paula.

And no peeing on the way!

PAULA. I think I can make it next door.

VICTOR. I don't know, maybe I should carry you.

PAULA. Honey, those days are gone, too!

(*They all laugh.*)

VICTOR. I think so. Good night. We enjoyed it.

MIKE. Good night.

PAULA. Bye.

MELANIE. See you Monday, Paula! (*Shuts the door. They lean against the door.*) Whew! I'm tired.

MIKE. (*Crosses to table to get pad and pencil.*) Yeah, I'm exhausted. They wear me out. I think they would stay all night if we didn't shove them out the door.

MELANIE. God forbid. (*Looks at him, crosses to him, puts arms over his shoulders.*) You know, I'm a lucky woman. Even after twenty-three years of marriage – you're still all right.

MIKE. Aw, shucks.

(*They kiss. He crosses to table SLC to put pad and pencil away.*)

MELANIE. I don't know what I'd do if you were like Victor. He makes me feel very uncomfortable sometimes.

MIKE. Yeah, he can be a little abrasive. (*Crosses to shut window and sheers.*)

MELANIE. That's being kind.

MIKE. He's all right. Just rough around the edges. You know he had it pretty hard growing up – no mother… an alcoholic father…

MELANIE. I know, but he's an adult now, and should be capable of making better choices. I swear I don't know how Paula puts up with it.

MIKE. She dishes it out pretty well, herself.

MELANIE. Yes, but usually in defense. Besides, Victor's crude. He…

MIKE. Forget it, honey. Let's not dwell on them…we have

better things to do.

(He kisses her.)

MELANIE. Mike!

(He unbuttons her top blouse.)

Mike!

MIKE. What?

MELANIE. Don't you think we ought to go to the bedroom? Keith may be home any minute.

MIKE. It's just after midnight. He hasn't been home before one o'clock in the morning since his summer break started.

*(**MIKE** tickles her. She takes off, squealing. He follows her around the sofa. He catches her and pulls her down to the sofa towards him. They laugh, he pulls her to him.)*

Come here, you.

*(As they kiss, the door flies open. **KEITH BARNSWORTH**, and **RICKY GIACOBI** come in. They all freeze; **MIKE** throws **MELANIE** to the floor as he jumps up. **MIKE** grabs and holds a pillow in front.)*

KEITH. Whoa!

MIKE. *(Seeing **MELANIE** on the floor.)* Oh!

*(Helps her up. She tries to button up her shirt. They end up on either side of the sofa, **MELANIE** by the kitchen.)*

Keith! You're home early!

KEITH. Uh, yeah. *(Shuts the door.)* We were kinda tired, and…uh, we could come back later…

*(He and **RICKY** are stifling laughs.)*

MIKE. No, no. Stay. Hi Ricky. What's up?

*(**RICKY** and **KEITH** laugh.)*

I mean, how's everything?

RICKY. Good. It's all good.

MELANIE. That's nice…You boys want something to eat?

(She turns to the boys with her shirt buttoned crookedly.

The boys are really giggling now.)

I'll, uh, I'll just go into the kitchen. We have some little sausages left, and…uh….I'll go warm them up.

(She exits. **MIKE** *joins in laughter.)*

KEITH. Sorry, Dad.

MIKE. No problem. We were just straightening up around here. Your parents were over, Ricky.

RICKY. Oh? Good. I guess they're talking again, then?

MIKE. Well, they were – their usual selves. Straight out of *The Honeymooners*, huh?

RICKY. What?

MIKE. *The Honeymooners.* The old TV show with Jackie Gleason and Art Carney…never mind. I guess it was way before your time.

RICKY. I guess so.

KEITH. Who won Spades?

MIKE. We knocked their socks off. The women didn't have a chance.

MELANIE. *(Entering, correctly buttoned.)* What's this?

MIKE. Just telling the guys about dominating the Spades game.

MELANIE. *(Crossing to boys.)* Did he happen to mention how we buried them at Catch Phrase?

MIKE. I was just getting to that.

MELANIE. I bet. So boys, what brings you in so early?

KEITH. We were, um, tired.

MELANIE. *(Studying them.)* You look tired. Are you all right?

KEITH. Yeah. Fine…a little hungry.

MELANIE. The sausages should be hot soon.

KEITH. Good. Thanks. So – uh, we'll go on into the kitchen…

*(**KEITH** motions to **RICKY** with head towards kitchen. **RICKY**, obliviously motions the other way. **KEITH** motions again, vehemently.)*

You guys go on with whatever you were doing...

*(He and **RICKY** laugh and scoot off to the kitchen as **MIKE** throws the pillow at them.)*

MIKE. Jealous!

MELANIE. *(Crosses and picks up pillow.)* Really, Mike.

*(**MIKE** comes behind her and tickles her.)*

MIKE! *(She squeals.)* Shhhh!

MIKE. You're the one making the noise. *(He chases her around sofa.)*

MELANIE. Mike, stop it. Now stop! Listen...Mike! *(Laughing, guides **MIKE** to sit on sofa as he persists on tickling her.)* Listen to me, Mike! Really!

MIKE. *(He finally stops playing with her.)* Okay, okay.

MELANIE. Mike, did you see their eyes?

MIKE. Yeah.

MELANIE. Well?

MIKE. Well, what?

MELANIE. Do you think they've been – you know.

MIKE. What?

MELANIE. Come on, you know what I'm saying.

MIKE. Are you saying you think they may have been... ?

(He 'tokes,' like at a joint.)

MELANIE. Yes, you know I am.

MIKE. My guess would be yes.

MELANIE. Aren't you concerned?

MIKE. About what? *(Teasing her.)* Don't play 'Miss Innocent' with me. You remember our college days.

MELANIE. I try to forget. Especially that mullet you had!

MIKE. That's it!

(He starts tickling her again.)

MELANIE. *(She shrieks.)* Ssshhh! *(Laughing.)* I'm not kidding. Stop! They'll hear us, Mike!

MIKE. Stop what?

MELANIE. You're trying to avoid the subject, and it's not going to work.

(He stops.)

I think you should say something to Keith. Just because we were irresponsible a …couple of times doesn't mean he can be. I want him to be better than we were.

MIKE. He's human, Mel. He's going to make his own choices, and his own mistakes.

MELANIE. This is one mistake he doesn't need to make. He's twenty-one now. He can drink himself into oblivion – he doesn't need to toke into it!

MIKE. That's good. Let's encourage him to drink himself into a stupor, just because he can.

MELANIE. You know that's not what I mean. But at least alcohol is legal.

MIKE. I'll talk to him about it. But who knows? Maybe we're wrong. Maybe they are just tired…

(At his last word, **KEITH** *and* **RICKY** *enter, hands full. A box of Ding Dongs, plate of sausages, Little Debbie Snacks, crackers, etc. and drinks. To* **MELANIE.***)*

I'll talk to him tomorrow.

KEITH. Talk to him who?

MELANIE. Never mind. You two enjoy. We're going to bed.

KEITH. You two enjoy, too!

*(***KEITH** *and* **RICKY** *giggle.)*

MELANIE. *(She stops and smiles.)* Make sure you clean up your mess.

KEITH. We will.

MELANIE. Good night, boys.

RICKY. Goodnight, Mrs. B. And thanks for the food.

MELANIE. Don't mention it.

(She exits. **MIKE** *starts out.)*

MIKE. Keith, how 'bout some one-on-one in the morning?

KEITH. Sounds good. But not too early.

MIKE. Right.

(He exits. The boys eat continually throughout the following.)

RICKY. You know how lucky you are?

KEITH. Lucky?

RICKY. Your parents. It's cool to see they still love each other.

KEITH. Yeah. Embarrassing, too.

RICKY. No, man. They really do. Laughing and screwing around like that – I mean – not – well, you know what I mean.

KEITH. Yeah, I know. Your parents aren't like that?

RICKY. Are you kidding? My parents hardly speak to each other. I thought they'd get divorced when I went to college, but they just hang on. To what, I don't know.

KEITH. There must be something there.

RICKY. Yeah, must be. Hey, how about some of those sausages?

KEITH. *(As they eat.)* How did you like that redhead playing pool at Jerry's Bar?

RICKY. She was okay.

KEITH. Okay? She was hot! What's the matter with you?

RICKY. Nothing's the matter with me. She just didn't do it for me.

KEITH. You didn't think she was hot.

RICKY. If junior high is hot, she was hot. I liked the woman at the bar.

KEITH. What?! She had to be at least thirty-five years old. I bet she was forty! Uh! *(He shudders.)*

RICKY. No way.

KEITH. Rick – that lady was pushing the top of the hill.

RICKY. Big frickin' deal! You like the ones still in diapers. I like classier women.

KEITH. If anyone's in diapers, it's the grandma you're hot over.

RICKY. Let's just say, the older they are, the more experienced they are. There's nothing wrong with *that*.

KEITH. Oh, really. And how would you know?

RICKY. Just take my word for it.

KEITH. Unh-uh. You gotta tell me, Ricky. You can't make a statement like that and then just sit on it.

RICKY. I…I can't. *(Takes the last Ding Dong from the box.)*

KEITH. You're just messin' with me.

RICKY. No, it's…let's just say, it's a delicate situation.

KEITH. Oh, come on. You gotta spill it. You can't back down from this now. *(Grabs Ding Dong from* **RICKY.***)* No Ding Dong till ya do.

RICKY. *(He tries to grab Ding Dong, from* **KEITH,** *to no avail.)* Okay. But I don't want it out there. You can't tell anyone.

KEITH. What do you think I'm gonna do…go on MySpace and tell the world? My best friend boinks old ladies.

(He pushes playfully at **RICKY.***)*

Come on!

*(***RICKY*** opens his mouth, then shakes his head.)*

Come ON!

RICKY. If I tell you – you gotta swear you won't breathe a word.

KEITH. I swear! I swear on…*(Looks around, holds up Ding Dong, becomes reverent.)* I swear on – the Ding Dong. I promise I will never tell a living, breathing soul, as long as I live, so help me Little Debbie.

RICKY. I guess I can't ask for more than that…Western Lit.

KEITH. What does Western Literature have to do with it?

RICKY. Think about it, Dilbert.

KEITH. *(It dawns on him.)* Oh my god!

RICKY. More like goddess!

KEITH. *(He's all over the place.)* Oh my god! You've been doin' our Western Lit teacher? Ms. Joyce?

RICKY. Shut up! Your parents will hear you! *(Throws a pillow* *at* **KEITH.**)

KEITH. Oh my god! She is hot.

RICKY. Yeah, she's hot. And she knows what she's doing.

KEITH. Details, you gotta give me details.

RICKY. Not on your life! Ding Dong, please.

(**KEITH** *gives him the Ding Dong.*)

Top that with your junior high redhead.

KEITH. Man…How old is Ms. Joyce, anyway?

RICKY. I don't know. We aren't that close.

KEITH. You're having sex with her, but you aren't close enough to know how old she is?

RICKY. It hasn't come up in our conversation. We don't talk much.

KEITH. What kind of relationship is that?

RICKY. I didn't say we were having a relationship. Just relations.

KEITH. Whatever works for you, but in the long run, I'm looking for something more than that. I'm gonna get to know that little redhead.

RICKY. In the *long run*, she's here, you're in college, and if you get into a relationship, someone's eventually going to get hurt.

KEITH. What about you and Ms. Joyce?

RICKY. Her name is Rebecca.

KEITH. Rebecca. Good. You know her first name, at least. Somebody's gonna get hurt in that situation, too. It's unavoidable.

RICKY. No it isn't. We aren't connected like that. We're in it for pleasure. Not promises.

KEITH. That can't be healthy.

RICKY. Healthy or not, that's what it is. And until summer's over, my pleasure's gonna come from 'Mary Jane'. (*Splits Ding Dong in half, addresses each half as 'Mary' and 'Jane', then stuffs both halves in his mouth.*) Oh my god.

KEITH. We're pathetic! Here we are, home at midnight on a Saturday night, stoned and eating Ding Dongs. Sure,

'Mary Jane' is all right, but she won't keep you warm at night, and you can't bring her home to momma.

RICKY. I could.

KEITH. That was the end of the bag, anyway – wait a minute. What do you mean, you could?

RICKY. I tell my mom everything.

KEITH. How sweet.

RICKY. It's not like that, ass wipe. I've just always been open with her.

KEITH. You gonna tell her about Ms. Joyce?

RICKY. Hell, no! Okay, so I don't tell her everything. But I could tell her I smoked pot. Not my dad, of course. He'd kick my ass.

KEITH. Yeah, mine probably would, too.

RICKY. Oh, I'm not saying Mom would approve. She'd just be cool about it and tell me not to do it again. We're open with *each other.*

KEITH. What do you mean?

RICKY. Well…never mind.

KEITH. No, what?

RICKY. She confides in me – about Dad. He doesn't always treat her right.

KEITH. Oh.

RICKY. I'm not saying he's abusive. Not in the 'beat the crap outta ya' sense. But he's, well, I guess he is mentally abusive…sometimes. I used to think he was just tough. But since I've been studying psychology, I've realized that it's more than that. Maybe some day he'll change…with therapy…lots of it. But I can just see him agreeing to *that.*

(Silence.)

Let's get this stuff cleaned up. I gotta get home.

KEITH. Sure.

(They pick up food and exit to kitchen. **RICKY** *accidentally drops a cracker on the floor before exiting. There's*

a rap on the door, handle wiggles, it slowly opens, and **PAULA** *enters. She has been crying.)*

PAULA. Melanie? You still up?

(She looks around, sees lights are on, heads towards kitchen.)

Melanie?

(Just as she gets to the door, **RICKY** *and* **KEITH** *enter. They all jump and shout.)*

Ricky! Keith! You scared the life out of me.

RICKY. What are you doing here, Mom?

PAULA. I – I was just looking for Melanie.

RICKY. This late?

KEITH. She went to bed.

PAULA. Oh…I'll leave then. *(Starts out.)*

RICKY. Wait a minute, Mom. What's going on?

PAULA. Nothing. I…I wanted to borrow a book from her…I couldn't sleep.

RICKY. Bullshit, Mom.

PAULA. Ricky….

RICKY. Mom. What happened? You've been crying!

PAULA. Nonsense, Ricky…*(Stuffs tissue in her pocket.)* I'm fine. I…it's nothing…

RICKY. What did Dad say this time?

PAULA. Please, Ricky. Not now.

RICKY. It's okay, Mom. Keith is my best friend. He knows.

PAULA. Ricky, you shouldn't burden him with our problems.

RICKY. Mom…

PAULA. Your dad and I had a little disagreement, that's all.

RICKY. About what?

PAULA. I'm not going to talk about it now. I'm going home. Good night, Keith. I'm sorry I disturbed you.

KEITH. You didn't. Really. I hope you'll be okay.

PAULA. I'll be fine. *(Starts out.)*

RICKY. I'm going with you. Bye, Keith. See you tomorrow.

> *(RICKY starts out. PAULA exits.)*

KEITH. Bye.

> *(KEITH goes into the kitchen to get water and turn out the light.)*

RICKY. Oh my god!

> *(He sees dropped cracker on the floor, picks it up, blows it off, and eats it as he exits.)*
>
> *(MIKE enters in robe and pajama pants, crosses towards the kitchen. He gets to the door just as KEITH enters the room, startles, and splashes water on MIKE.)*

MIKE. Oh! What the...

KEITH. I'm sorry. You scared me. *(Runs into kitchen for towel.)*

MIKE. *I* scared *you!*

KEITH. *(Runs back with towel.)* Here.

MIKE. Thanks. I needed a shower. What was all the commotion out here?

KEITH. Paula came over.

MIKE. Why?

KEITH. She and Victor had a fight.

MIKE. Oh. Yeah, they don't get along too well sometimes.

KEITH. That's what Ricky said.…Thanks, Dad.

MIKE. For what?

KEITH. For being cool.

MIKE. I'm not *that* cool. I am still the Dad.

KEITH. I know. But you treat Mom right. And me.

MIKE. I love ya.

KEITH. I know. Me, too.…Well, I guess I'll head off to bed.

MIKE. Uh, Keith?

KEITH. Yeah?

MIKE. There's… uh, there's something I want to talk to you about.

KEITH. What's that?

MIKE. An evil woman.

KEITH. What?

MIKE. 'Mary Jane?'

KEITH. Oh.

MIKE. She's not good for you, you know.

KEITH. I know.

MIKE. So…?

KEITH. I don't often. Not much.

MIKE. That's good. How much is not much?

KEITH. A few times…uh, a guy at school gave me a bag.

MIKE. He gave you a *bag*?

KEITH. I guess a half a bag.

MIKE. He gave it to you because he wants to sell you more.

KEITH. I know, Dad. But I'm not buying any.

MIKE. I hope not.

KEITH. You know, it's not addicting. Not like alcohol is.

MIKE. No substance is good for you if it alters your mind, son. A drink or two socially, that's fine. But don't ever become too attached to any of it. You gotta stay in control of that mind of yours. Especially since it's taking so much of my bank account to educate it! *(He ruffles* **KEITH***'s head.)*

KEITH. Right.

MIKE. Right. Well, that's the end of my public service announcement.

KEITH. You know, Dad, you're a real dork sometimes.

MIKE. What?

KEITH. An evil woman! That's really dorky.

MIKE. So I'm a big dork. This dork is gonna kick your butt on the court tomorrow.

(They start towards archway.)

KEITH. In your dreams, old man, in your dreams.

*(***MIKE*** turns out light as they exit.)*

Scene 2

(The following Monday night, almost seven o'clock. The doorbell rings. **PAULA**, *carrying a dish and a duffle bag, looks in. Enters, sets bag by the door, crosses to sofa.)*

PAULA. Hellooo…Melanie? It's me.

MELANIE. *(Sticking her head out of the kitchen door.)* Make yourself at home. I'll be finished in a minute.

PAULA. I brought spinach dip. *(She sets dish on table.)*

MELANIE *(Offstage.)* Great!

PAULA. It's almost seven, Mel.

MELANIE *(Offstage.)* Can you turn on the TV?

PAULA. Okay.

(She looks for remote, finds it under a sofa cushion, but doesn't turn it on yet.)

*(***MIKE*** enters with baseball shirt and shorts on, as* ***MELANIE*** *comes out of the kitchen with snacks and drinks, wearing a big shirt and knit pants. She crosses to coffee table and sets snacks down.)*

MIKE. Hey, Paula. Ready for the big night?

PAULA. You know it. Oh, Victor asked me to tell you he'd meet you at the game. He's running late at the office.

MIKE. If he hasn't left yet, he won't make it home in time to change and get to the field.

PAULA. Oh, I almost forgot, I brought his gear over. Can you take it to him? It's by the door.

MIKE. Uh, I – Sure. *(Crossing to front door.)* All right, I'm off. Have fun, ladies.

MELANIE. *(Crossing to him.)* You, too. Hit a homer for me!

MIKE. Will do.

(They kiss.)

PAULA. Bye, Mike. *(Turns on TV.)*

MELANIE. Bye.

MIKE. Bye, hon. Love ya! *(Exits, shutting door.)*

(SFX: Theme song for Facing Facts.)

PAULA. It's on, Melanie.

MELANIE. Okay, okay. *(She crosses to sofa.)*

PAULA *(Overlapping music.)* I'm so excited! I can't wait to see who's going to be on!

FRANCES. *(Voice over.)* Hello, America! Welcome to tonight's edition of *Facing Facts.*

MELANIE *(Speaking over television.)* I still can't believe they're in our hometown!

FRANCES. *(Voice over.)* I am your host, Frances Montgomery, and tonight we're going to a quaint little suburb of our beautiful city. There we will confront a woman who has completely let herself go. We will help her to face the fact that she has gone from a slim, beautiful woman, to a plump little house frau.

MELANIE. I would die.

PAULA. I know!

FRANCES. *(Voice over.)* You know whom I'm talking about. She got her man, now she's got a belly the size of Georgia.

*(***PAULA*** and ***MELANIE*** gasp simultaneously.)*

She might claim, "It's that horrible baby fat that never went away." But we know the score, don't we? It's laziness! It's failure to exercise! It's pigging out! Now we all know the only way to keep your man is to keep your figure. Right? Right! So stay tuned....It's going to be an exciting episode.

*(***MELANIE*** hits mute.)*

MELANIE. My god. She is vicious tonight.

PAULA. She's a hoot! I pity the poor woman she's going to assault this time.

MELANIE. No kidding! Oh! I almost forgot. *(She stands and crosses to kitchen.)*

PAULA. What'd you forget?

MELANIE. You'll see. I bought something special since it's almost my birthday.

PAULA. Your birthday is two months away.

MELANIE. That's almost enough for me. (*She exits.*)

PAULA. Hurry up. I think the commercials are almost over. How do you turn this mute thing back on?

(*SFX: The phone rings.*)

Damn it, now she's going to miss the next part. Call them back!

(*She messes with the remote, finds her reading glasses, and finally turns off mute button. SFX: Theme song for Facing Facts.* PAULA *watches TV, it's fuzzy. She realizes her reading glasses are still on, takes them off. Looks towards the kitchen.*)

Hurry up!

(*She looks back at the TV and recognizes the sidewalk* FRANCES *is walking up. She freezes, wide-eyed, stunned.*)

MELANIE (*Speaking over television.*) I'll be right there. Wrong number.

FRANCES. (*Voice over.*) Welcome back to *Facing Facts*! As you can see, we're heading up the sidewalk of the lucky lady whose life we're about to change forever.

(PAULA *is frozen.* FRANCES *rings* MELANIE*'s doorbell.*)

MELANIE. Would you get that, Paula?

(PAULA *shakes her head 'No!'.*)

FRANCES. (*Voice over.*) She's not coming to the door! I know she's home. My assistant just rang her phone, and pretended to be a wrong number. Let's go in.

(PAULA *is in silent shock as* MELANIE *enters with a bag of Pinwheel cookies.* PAULA *slowly turns to* MELANIE *as the door begins to open.* PAULA *is dumbstruck.*)

MELANIE. My favorite! Pinwheels!

(*She takes a big bite out of one. It's still hanging from her mouth as the front door opens. The cameraperson,*

BOZ, *comes in backwards to wall, followed by* **FRANCES** *who stops center.)*

FRANCES. Hello, Melanie Barnsworth! Congratulations! You are on *Facing Facts*!

*(***MELANIE*** looks at* **FRANCES***, then the TV, and dives down, crawling in front of the coffee table toward the arch.* **BOZ** *crosses towards her, and keeps the camera on* **MELANIE**. **FRANCES** *runs around left side of sofa, stopping* **MELANIE**. **MONICA** *enters with make-up case, etc. and steps behind dining room table.* **MIKE** *comes to front door, with* **MELANIE**'s *suitcase in hand.* **MELANIE** *doesn't see him.)*

Oh, no, you don't, Mrs. Barnsworth. You can't get away from the truth, and you certainly can't get away from our camera.

(The camera is right on **MELANIE**'s *butt as she tries to crawl away.* **FRANCES** *kneels in front of* **MELANIE**, *and is face to face with her.)*

So tell me, Melanie, isn't it time you began facing facts?

*(***MELANIE*** spits the Pinwheel cookie hitting* **FRANCES** *in the face.)*

OH!

*(***FRANCES*** looks towards camera.)*

Perhaps it's time for a word from our sponsor. We'll be right back after these messages.

(The camera goes down. **FRANCES** *jumps up.)*

MAKEUP! Boz! Turn off their TV!

*(***FRANCES*** crosses toward* **MONICA**. **BOZ** *crosses to remote and turns TV off.* **MIKE** *crosses towards* **MELANIE**.*)*

Make sure she didn't screw up my face.

*(***MONICA*** rubs* **FRANCES**' *cheek.)*

MIKE. Melanie, what are you doing on the floor?

*(He starts helping **MELANIE** up from the floor. **MELANIE** is in shock.)*

FRANCES. Ouch! Don't rub so hard.

MONICA. Sorry. There's a bit of chocolate on your cheek.

MIKE. Melanie...

FRANCES. The things I go through for these people. Check my lips, too.

MONICA. Yes, Ma'am.

MIKE. Melanie!

MELANIE. *(Stunned.)* Mike? What are you doing here?

MIKE. Are you all right?

MELANIE. All right? All right! No, I'm not ALL RIGHT! I have just been humiliated on national television!

MIKE. But I thought that's what you wanted!

MELANIE. You thought I wanted to be humiliated on national television?!

MIKE. No – I –

FRANCES. *(To **MIKE** and **MELANIE**.)* Save it for the camera. We'll be back on in a minute. *(To **MONICA**, who is still messing with her hair.)* For heaven's sake that's enough.

MONICA. Yes, ma'am.

FRANCES. And bring me a bottle of water. HURRY! We're almost on.

BOZ. In ten seconds.

*(**MONICA** starts back with bottled water. **FRANCES** starts crossing back to **MIKE** and **MELANIE**.)*

FRANCES. *(to **MONICA**.)* Forget it. You're too slow!

BOZ. And we're on in five, four, three…

FRANCES. *(Pushing **MELANIE** back down at four count.)* Get back down! Down!

*(**BOZ** motions to go at silent one beat.)*

And we're back with Mrs. Melanie Barnsworth.

*(She stoops to help **MELANIE** back up.)*

Come, dear, let me help you up. There, there we go. Tell me, Melanie, are you ready to face the facts?

(**MELANIE** *stares at her.*)

You're just too overwhelmed to even speak, aren't you? Bless your poor little heart. Well, let me tell you, this wonderful, handsome husband of yours sent us a very special letter.

(*Turns* **MELANIE** *toward* **MIKE**.)

MELANIE. A letter?

(**MIKE** *grins and nods.*)

FRANCES. She speaks, ladies and gentlemen! Yes, Melanie, a letter. Stating how much you love our show, *Facing Facts*. That's right, isn't it, Mike?

MIKE. (*Stilted.*) Yes. That is right. She watches every Monday night with her best friend, Paula Giacobi.

(*He points to* **PAULA**, *who puts a pillow over her face.*)

FRANCES. Melanie.

(**MELANIE** *is staring at* **MIKE** *now.*)

MELANIE!

(**MELANIE** *startled, turns back to* **FRANCES**.)

Melanie, Mike told us how unhappy you are with your weight problem. How ashamed you are to have let yourself get so out of control. He also told us how much you love the beautiful tropical resort – where we send those who are fortunate enough to be chosen to be on *Facing Facts*. Where you learn to cook and eat properly, exercise efficiently, and get your life back in control. He thinks it's just the thing you need to help you get back on track to a healthy life style and a beautiful body.

MELANIE. He said that? (*To* **MIKE**.) You said that?

MIKE. Well, not…

FRANCES. Of course he did. He loves you. And he wants you to be the beautiful person he once knew. The woman he married.

(**KEITH** *enters the house.*)

MELANIE. I can't believe this is happening.

FRANCES. Yes. It is unbelievable, isn't it?

KEITH. What's going on here?

FRANCES. And who is this handsome young man? (*She grabs* **MELANIE**'s *hand and drags her to the door.*)

MELANIE. What? Oh, him. That's my son. Keith.

FRANCES. So he's the one who caused all that baby fat? My, he's a little old for you to still be blaming him for those fluffy handles around your waist, now, isn't he?

MELANIE. I never said…

FRANCES. Melanie, it's time to face the facts. (*In baby tone.*) Mellie's belly isn't from baby fat.

MELANIE. I didn't…

(**MELANIE** *points toward* **KEITH**. **FRANCES** *grabs her hand with her finger still pointing.*)

FRANCES. Uh, uh, uh. You did. It's time for you to put the blame where it belongs. It's time to face the facts and point that finger at – yourself.

(*She points* **MELANIE**'s *finger at* **MELANIE**, *then gives* **MELANIE** *a big hug. Looks into camera.*)

We'll be right back with more – but soon to be less of Mrs. Melanie Barnsworth. (*Big smile, and drops it.*) That was all right, Melanie, but you should act a little more ashamed. You're just standing there with your mouth wide open.

(*She pops* **MELANIE**'s *mouth shut, then walks toward* **MONICA**.)

Monica! Where is my water!?

MIKE. Melanie…

(*He reaches out to* **MELANIE**, *but she turns away.*)

(**MONICA** *has been staring at* **KEITH**. *He turns as* **FRANCES** *passes him, and catches* **MONICA**'s *eye. She is* *the redhead from the bar.)*

FRANCES. Monica!

MONICA. Oh, I'm sorry. Here, Ms. Montgomery.

(FRANCES jerks the water from MONICA as she crosses past her.)

FRANCES. Thank you so much!

MIKE. Melanie!

KEITH. Hey, weren't you at Jerry's Bar Saturday night?

MONICA. Yeah. I saw you there.

KEITH. I saw you, too.

MIKE. Melanie. Please, talk to me.

MELANIE. *(She reels on him.)* You want me to talk to you? About what, Mike? About how fat I am? About how lazy I am? About how beautiful I used to be?!

FRANCES. Hey! I told you – save it for the camera!

MIKE. I never said those things.

MELANIE. Then what are they doing here? In my house! Invading my life?!

MIKE. I thought you would be excited. It's your favorite show!

MELANIE. Not anymore!!

MIKE. *(Turning to PAULA.)* Paula. Help me.

PAULA. Sorry. You're on your own with this one.

BOZ. Ten seconds!

FRANCES. Damn it! Here!

(She pushes water bottle at MONICA, pushing her into KEITH.)

BOZ. In five, four, three…

(Points to FRANCES just as she gets to MIKE.)

FRANCES. We're back now, talking with Melanie's handsome, loving husband, Mike Barnsworth. *(She caresses his arm, and he's a little taken.)* So, Mike, tell us, how have you coped all these years, as you watched your wife balloon out of control?

(MELANIE looks at her, bewildered.)

MIKE. I just...Well, she didn't...uh, what was the question?

FRANCES. Isn't he adorable! I could just eat him up. Don't you worry, Mister. We're going to get your chunky little wife back into shape before you can even miss her.

MELANIE. You're what?

FRANCES. You heard right, Melanie. You are going away...

(FRANCES tries to pull MELANIE towards the camera, but MELANIE stalls. FRANCES tugs at MELANIE, and finally she follows her.)

You are going away to our fantastic tropical spa – for four entire weeks! And when you get back, you will be well on your way to becoming the woman you used to be. The woman your husband will once again be *proud* to be seen with – the new and improved Mrs. Melanie Barnsworth.

MELANIE. But, but, but...

(FRANCES covers MELANIE's mouth.)

FRANCES. No need to thank us, dear. That's why we're here – to help you face the facts and lose the fat.

(FRANCES thumps MELANIE's stomach.)

Your thoughtful husband has packed your bag, and your chariot awaits right outside the door. *(Turns to camera.)* And now, stay tuned as *Facing Facts*' very own Joey Montego interviews Dilly Pierce, the man who couldn't turn down a donut. I think you'll be surprised at the metamorphosis that took place in only four short weeks. Perhaps Melanie Barnsworth will be our next successful makeover – and remember...it's never too late for – *Facing Facts*. I'm Frances Montgomery, until next time! *(She blows a kiss to the camera.)*

BOZ. And we're out.

FRANCES. Thank god. That was a tough one, but I'm sure it played well. *(Turns to MELANIE.)* It's time to say your goodbyes, Melanie. We'll be waiting for you. And Mike...*(She caresses his chest, as he backs into the wall.)*

It was simply scrumptious to meet you. You are quite charming.

MIKE. It's been great meeting you, too. Thank you.

(**FRANCES** *slides her hand off as she crosses toward the door.*)

FRANCES. Monica.

KEITH. (*To* **MONICA**, *quietly.*) Maybe I'll catch you at Jerry's Bar again.

MONICA. I hope so. Bye for-

FRANCES. MONICA!

(**MONICA** *jumps, and runs out the door and opens it for* **FRANCES**.)

(*Everyone is quiet until the door closes.* **MELANIE** *looks at* **MIKE**. *She takes a deep breath, crosses toward* **PAULA** *who stands and crosses towards her.*)

MELANIE. Goodbye, Paula. Take care. (*They hug. She crosses to* **KEITH**.) Bye, sweetie. I'll miss you. I love you. (*She hugs him and kisses his cheek.*)

KEITH. I love you, too, Mom. And you're not...

MELANIE. (*She puts her hand on his mouth.*) It's okay. Would you two leave us alone for a minute please?

PAULA. Sure. We'll just get some water. Have fun?

(**MELANIE** *nods.* **PAULA** *and* **KEITH** *exit.*)

MIKE. Melanie, I – (*Crosses to* **MELANIE**. *She holds her hand up.*)

MELANIE. Don't. (*She pauses.*) Mike, I thought...I thought we had a good life together.

MIKE. We do –

MELANIE. Please. Let me speak.

MIKE. But you won't hear me out.

MELANIE. There is nothing you can say that will ever help me understand why you did this to me.

MIKE. I...

MELANIE. No! I have to say this now, because thanks to you, I have to leave my home...I have never been so completely mortified...I know I am a big woman. I have constantly struggled with my weight – and my self-esteem. I've had to deal with it for the last twenty years of my life. I'm sorry – I didn't realize it has been so hard for you to deal with, too.

MIKE. I never...

MELANIE. Please, let me finish. It took a long time for me to finally come to terms with the way I am, and to love myself for who I am, and not to...obsess...about how I look. And in a few minutes, which felt like an eternity, you completely destroyed that. But the worst part... *(Choking back tears.)* The worst part is, I thought you loved me. I thought you loved *me*!

MIKE. I did. I do!

MELANIE. Then how could you say those things?

MIKE. I didn't. Not the way Frances put it.

MELANIE. No? Then why didn't you say something tonight? You just let her go on insulting me. You stood there like Bambi caught in headlights!

MIKE. She wouldn't let me say anything.

MELANIE. Oh, you had the opportunity. You were just too star-struck to speak.

MIKE. Well, I'm sorry, but it isn't every day you're on national television.

MELANIE. No kidding! So is that why you let her paw all over you, too?

MIKE. Give me a break, Melanie. What am I supposed to do? Deck the hostess?

MELANIE. You're supposed to take up for me!

MIKE. I *tried* to!

MELANIE. Not hard enough.

(She starts towards the door. He stops her.)

MIKE. Wait a minute, Melanie. You aren't being fair! You're not even considering the fact that I did this for *you*. You and Paula watch Facing Facts all the time. You talk about it all the time. I was trying to do something nice for you! And instead of thanking me, you kick me in the gut! I mean – how am I supposed to know what you want?

MELANIE. I'll tell you what I want...what I want is for you to be out of the house when I get back.

MIKE. Now you're being irrational. You don't mean that.

MELANIE. Yes, Mike. I do. *(She crosses to door.)*

MIKE. Melanie.

MELANIE. *(She picks up suitcase and opens door, turns back.)* It doesn't take four weeks to change your life. It only takes a moment. *(She exits.)*

MIKE. Melanie...Melanie!

(MIKE closes door, looks around room, trying to figure out what happened. He crosses to sofa, and sits, face in hands. PAULA peeks in, sees MIKE is alone, and enters with KEITH.)

PAULA. She's gone? *(She crosses to him and sits.)*

MIKE. Yeah.

KEITH. What happened, Dad?

MIKE. *(Shakes his head.)* I only wanted her to be happy. *(To PAULA.)* I thought this would make her happy, Paula.

PAULA. I know.

MIKE. Paula, you and Melanie love *Facing Facts*. We were all talking about it Saturday night. She said the spa is fabulous! 'What a way to help you get into shape!' She said that! Didn't she?

PAULA. Yes.

MIKE. I don't understand her reaction. I thought she would be thrilled...

PAULA. It's just...*Facing Facts* is entertaining...when you see it on television...when you watch the turmoil that Frances Montgomery puts those people through. It isn't quite so entertaining when you realize it's real people she's hurting. When it's you.

MIKE. I never would have...if I had known what it's really like…I never would have sent that letter. I love her, Paula!

PAULA. I know. It'll be all right.

MIKE. No, it won't. She wants me out.

KEITH. She didn't say that, Dad.

MIKE. Yes, she did, Keith. She wants me gone when she gets back.

KEITH. She'll be gone four weeks – she'll change her mind. You know she will. Mom can never stay mad at you.

MIKE. Yeah. But she isn't just mad. I've hurt her. And that's the *worst* thing I could do.

(He stands and exits to bedroom as **PAULA** *and* **KEITH** *watch.)*

(Lights out.)

Scene 3

(It's a Friday around 6:30, almost four weeks later. The lights are out. Keys jingle outside the front door; **MIKE** *enters wearing a suit. He's lookIng at the mail.* **KEITH** *is on the sofa, but* **MIKE** *doesn't see him.* **MIKE** *sniffs the air.)*

MIKE. Melanie? *(There's no answer.)* That's her perfume. *(Not moving, he looks around.)* I'm losing my mind! *(He shakes his head as he exits through the arch.)* God help me.

*(***MONICA** *pops up from the couch, from behind* **KEITH**. *She straightens her clothes some.)*

MONICA. That was close. I would be so embarrassed if he caught us.

KEITH. Yeah. It'd be kinda funny though.

MONICA. Funny? I don't think so.

KEITH. Yeah, it would. I caught my parents a few weeks ago.

MONICA. You're kidding! How?

KEITH. Right here on this couch.

MONICA. No!

KEITH. Yeah! A friend and I came in one night – in fact it was the night I first saw you – and they were going at it on the couch.

MONICA. Oh my god! I would totally die!

KEITH. I think my mom almost did. But it was really funny.

MONICA. *(Rises to get lip-gloss from purse.)* I think I'd go into a coma if I ever walked in on my parents. But then they pretty much live in a vegetative state.

KEITH. Yeah? My parents aren't like that. I should say weren't. I don't know what's going to happen with them now.

MONICA. I'm so sorry your mom had to go through all that on the show. Frances can be such a nasty skank.

KEITH. How can you stand working with her?

MONICA. I can't! But this internship is a steppingstone.

Someday, I hope to produce and direct decent television – or movies.

KEITH. As a make-up artist?

MONICA. No. I'm a film major at school. *(Playfully pushes him.)* I told you that.

KEITH. Oh, that's right. Now I remember.

MONICA. Very funny! *(He kisses her.)* You're forgiven.

*(They kiss again as **MIKE** enters the room, coat jacket and tie off.)*

MIKE. *(Startled, then sniffing.)* So that's where the perfume came from.

KEITH. *(Breaking away from **MONICA**.)* Dad. You remember Monica – from *Facing Facts?*

MIKE. Monica? I remember the face. *(Crosses to shake her hand.)* Sorry, I'm not too good with names. It's nice to see you again.

MONICA. Hello, Mr. Barnsworth. How are you?

MIKE. Much better now that I know I'm not losing my mind. Nice perfume. Forever, right?

MONICA. Yeah. Thanks.

MIKE. It's the perfume my wife wears.

MONICA. Oh. I'm so sorry.

MIKE. No – it's not your fault. It's nice to smell it again. Reminds me of her. So how did you two hook up? Did you meet here?

KEITH. No. Actually we met – well, saw each other – at Jerry's Bar the Saturday before. Then the night of the show – well, there she was, and…it was fate, I guess.

MIKE. That was a fateful night, all right.

MONICA. *(Blurting out.)* Mr. Barnsworth, I am so sorry. Ms. Montgomery can be so cruel. She puts words in people's mouths, and exaggerates to the point of lying. She has absolutely no empathy. All she cares about are the ratings. She has no sense of decency to others. She's a soulless witch that should rot in hell for what she did to you and your wife.

KEITH. Tell us how you really feel.

MONICA. *(Embarrassed.)* Oh! I – well –*(Shrugs, then matter of factly.)* That's how I really feel.

MIKE. I appreciate your empathy, Monica, but ultimately it was my fault. I sent the letter. Now I just have to figure out how to get out of the mess I got myself into.

MONICA. I wish I could do something to help.

MIKE. There is something. How is Melanie doing? Is she happy at the resort?

MONICA. I don't know. I never get to go there. I only go on Ms. Montgomery's ambushes. And sometimes when she does the interviews after the makeovers, but that's usually Joey Montego.

MIKE. I see. Thanks, anyway. Hey, you two kids hungry? Our fridge is loaded. Our neighbor, Paula – she brings food over constantly since Melanie's been gone.

KEITH. Paula's a great cook. I think I've gained ten pounds.

MONICA. Thanks for the invite, but we're having dinner with my parents tonight. Oh, I better call and let them know we'll meet them at the restaurant. *(Pulls cell phone from purse, stops.)* Oh, I forgot my battery is dead. Can I use your phone?

MIKE. *(Points to the kitchen.)* Sure. It's in the kitchen.

MONICA. Thanks. I'll be right back. *(She exits.)*

MIKE. So – it's meet the parents night, huh? *(Nudges* **KEITH.** *)*

KEITH. Yeah. I'm nervous.

MIKE. You are?

*(***KEITH*** nods.)*

You really like this girl?

KEITH. Yeah, I do. She's great. She gets me.

MIKE. There's a lot to be said for that, son. That's how your mom and I are – were.

KEITH. You'll be there again. When she gets home, things will be back to normal before you know it.

MIKE. I hope you're right. But it'll be hard to get there, if I'm not here.

KEITH. You aren't going anywhere, Dad.

MIKE. Keith, she wants me out of the house when she gets home.

KEITH. I don't believe that for a minute. When she gets back, she's gonna realize she wants you to stay. I bet you anything.

MIKE. No bet, son.

MONICA. *(Bopping back in.)* They're already on the way, Keith. We have to run. *(She crosses to door.)*

KEITH. *(Crosses to door,* **MIKE** *follows.)* Okay. See ya later, Dad.

MIKE. Have a good time, kids.

MONICA. *(She stops at door.)* It was nice to officially meet you, Mr. Barnsworth. I wish you peace. *(She solemnly touches his forehead, then is lively.)* Bye! *(She exits.)*

KEITH. *(Shrugs.)* Of course, I don't always get *her*, but I like it. *(He exits.)*

(**MIKE** *laughs as he closes the door. He untucks his dress shirt and unbuttons it most of the way as he crosses toward the bedroom. There is a banging on the door.)*

MIKE. Who's banging…? I'm coming!

(He opens the door. **PAULA** *is there, holding a big pot.)*

Hi, Paula. Come on in.

PAULA. Sorry. I would've let myself in, but my hands were full… here, I made you a pot roast. *(Hands pot to* **MIKE.***)*

MIKE. Thanks, Paula. *(Crosses to put pot on table.)* But you really didn't need to do that. Our refrigerator's never been so full.

PAULA. I guess I am overdoing it. It's just, well, I feel so badly for you and Melanie. I wish there was something more I could do, but comfort food is the only thing I know.

MIKE. You're the best, Paula. I appreciate everything... Listen, you have a minute?

PAULA. Sure. Victor won't be home for a while. He's working late again.

(They cross to sofa to sit.)

MIKE. Melanie comes home next week. Monday.

PAULA. Yes.

MIKE. She still isn't talking to me, Paula. I've called her everyday. Sometimes twice – even three times a day. The receptionist has me on speed answer – 'Hello. Mrs. Barnsworth is not available. Have a nice day.' Click....How can we ever get past this if she won't talk to me?

PAULA. I don't know, Mike. I've tried to talk to her about it. She won't listen. She refuses to talk about anything except the boys and the resort. If I bring you up, she suddenly has to go.

MIKE. She does the same thing to Keith. I can't understand this. I was trying to do a good thing, and in the process, I destroyed everything. Can you explain it?

PAULA. Well....no. I can't. Ricky's the psychology major. You'll have to ask him.

MIKE. Wow. Dr. Giacobi. Thanks for being such a good friend, Paula.

(They embrace on the sofa. Suddenly, the front door bangs open. **VICTOR** *is in a crazed state.)*

VICTOR. Aha! I caught you!

*(***MIKE*** and ***PAULA*** separate.)*

PAULA. Victor! What are you doing here? I thought you had to work late.

VICTOR. That's what I told you – so I could catch you in the act! *(He removes his blazer and starts rolling up his sleeves as he crosses down to* **MIKE.***)* I knew something was going on over here. Come on, Mike. We're gonna have this out.

MIKE. *(Standing.)* Now hold on, Victor. You have this all wrong.

PAULA. What's the matter with you, Victor?

VICTOR. What's the matter with me? What's the matter with you! Carrying on behind my back...look-it, he's half naked!

MIKE. What? *(Looks down, sees shirt unbuttoned. Starts to button it.)* Victor, listen... I was talking to –

PAULA. Let me handle this, Mike. *(She pushes past **MIKE** to **VICTOR**, who has his fists up.)* Now Victor...*(She starts to pat his arm, and grabs his thumb, bending it back.)*

VICTOR. *(Bending at his knees. Played comically.)* Ow, ow, ow, ow, okay, okay, I give...I give. Let go, already.

PAULA. Are you going to behave yourself?

VICTOR. Yeah.

PAULA. *(Pulls his thumb again.)* Victor...

VICTOR. Yeah, yeah, yeah.

PAULA. *(Letting him go.)* Victor, you know there's nothing going on between Mike and me. He is our friend – your best friend. I just brought him dinner.

VICTOR. Then what was all that on the couch, huh?

MIKE. I was talking to her about Melanie.

PAULA. I was consoling him. You ever heard of that word? It means to comfort!

VICTOR. I know what the damn word means. What am I, an idiot?

PAULA. If the shoe fits...

VICTOR. The fact is all this looks pretty fishy to me – you always comin' over here, bringing him food. You never cook that much for me at home!

PAULA. You don't need comforting. And you eat plenty at home. There's no denying that! *(Pops his belly.)*

MIKE. I think I'm gonna pop into the kitchen...

(They aren't listening to him. He exits into the kitchen.)

VICTOR. *(Over MIKE's line.)* What? Now you're callin' me fat? I ain't the fat one around here. I keep fit. I play ball every Monday night.

PAULA. Play ball? You're the catcher, for Pete's sake. How much exercise is that?

VICTOR. I bat. I even make it to second or third base sometimes – more often than I do at home!

PAULA. You and your stupid baseball metaphors….they're not that funny!

VICTOR. Oh, yeah? Well, your pot roast ain't that good!

PAULA. Now you're attacking my cooking? How can you attack my cooking? You love my cooking.

VICTOR. Yeah, well I can't even taste it most of the time, cause you're driving me nuts with your nagging. Always on my case…I can't do a damn thing right.

PAULA. I don't nag. I suggest!

VICTOR. Well, let me suggest this. DON'T!

PAULA. I can't believe we're even arguing about this. I came over here to console our dear friend, Mike…*(She turns and points to where MIKE was standing; he's not there.)* Mike? Where'd he go?

VICTOR. I don't know. He was there just a minute ago.

PAULA. He's hiding from us. You embarrassed him with your ridiculous accusations.

VICTOR. It wasn't my fault, you sneaking over here behind my back.

PAULA. There was nothing sneaky about it. I was…Oh, forget it. Just settle down.

VICTOR. I will if you will.

PAULA. Oh, grow up. *(Starts for kitchen.)* Mike? Mike, you in the kitchen?

(Just as she is crossing to the kitchen, MIKE comes out.)

MIKE. You two go to your corners?

PAULA. What?

VICTOR. That's one of those stupid sports metaphors.

Boxing.

PAULA. Oh. Gotcha. Sorry, Mike.

VICTOR. Yeah, no foul, huh, Mike?

MIKE. Don't worry about it. And listen…here. Take the pot roast home. *(Crossing to table to get pot.* **VICTOR** *and* **PAULA** *follow.)* I have a full fridge. Besides, I know how much you love it. He always raves about your pot roast, Paula.

PAULA. Oh, really?

VICTOR. No, you keep it. It's the least I can do.

PAULA. You can do?

VICTOR. Yeah. I paid for it.

MIKE. No, I insist.

(He hands them the pot as they continue their discussion.)

PAULA. I went to the grocery store. I put it in the pot to cook. I cut the potatoes, and the carrots…

VICTOR. But who earns the paycheck? Huh?… Who works Monday through Friday, eight to five…?

PAULA. Not me. I work every day of the week. You think the house cleans itself? You couldn't afford to pay someone to do what I do…Cook, clean, wash your stinking underwear…pick up your…

*(***VICTOR*** exits out the door as* **PAULA** *is speaking.)*

MIKE. Victor…

*(***VICTOR*** turns around and* **MIKE** *hands him his blazer.* **VICTOR** *grabs it and heads back out.* **PAULA** *finishes her line as she and* **VICTOR** *head out the door and down the walkway.)*

PAULA. …wet towels off the floor. Sometimes you irritate the hell out of me, Victor!

*(***MIKE*** shuts the door as they are still arguing, shakes his head and goes back to the kitchen. He enters with a bag of pretzels and a beer. He sits on the sofa, turns on the television and tosses the remote on the sofa. A promotion*

for Monday night's Facing Facts is on.)

MIKE *(Overlapping voice over.)* Oh, no. Not this!

(He looks for then grabs the remote to turn it off, just as he hears 'Ms. Melanie Barnsworth', he stops to watch, growing agitated.)

JOEY MONTEGO. *(Voice over.)* So don't miss the next exciting edition of *Facing Facts*, Monday night at seven o'clock, when I interview the lovely *Ms.* Melanie Barnsworth. You won't believe the amazing transformation that took place in only four short weeks, and neither will her family and friends. You'll also be right there with Frances Montgomery as she joins a family desperate to stop their son from shoplifting.

MIKE. *(Stands, points the clicker at the T.V., and speaks to the television.)* It's *Mrs.* Melanie Barnsworth! MRS. NOT MS.! It has been for twenty-three years, and it's going to stay that way, you bastard!

(He clicks off the television, and throws the remote on the sofa.)

(Fast lights out.)

ACT II

Scene 1

(It is almost seven o'clock, Monday night, four weeks after **MELANIE** *left.* **MIKE**, **KEITH**, **PAULA**, **VICTOR**, *and* **RICKY** *are waiting for* **MELANIE** *and the crew from Facing Facts to get there.* **KEITH**, **RICKY** *and* **VICTOR** *are eating a snack at the table.* **PAULA** *sits in the chair, anxiously waiting.* **MIKE** *paces behind the sofa.)*

MIKE. What time is it?

VICTOR. It's one minute later than the last time you asked.

MIKE. Well, what time is that?

VICTOR. It's 6:57.

MIKE. Oh my god. I'm gonna have a coronary.

PAULA. *(Stands.)* I'll get you some water.

MIKE. *(Stopping her.)* I don't want any water. I only want it to be 7:00.

PAULA. *(Looks at her watch.)* It will be in…two minutes. *(She nervously sits again, looking towards television.)*

MIKE. Two minutes. She's going to be here in two minutes. What is she going to do when she sees me?

KEITH. Calm down, Dad. She knows you have to be here for the interview. And she'll want you to stay.

MIKE. From your mouth to Melanie's ears. What time is it?

VICTOR. It's 6:58 – and a half.

MIKE. Keith, turn on the television. It's almost time.

RICKY. Hey, Keith, is Monica going to be here?

KEITH. *(Crossing to sofa to get remote.)* No. Joey Montego is coming for the interview. Monica has to go with Frances Montgomery. She's her assistant.

RICKY. That's too bad.

KEITH. Yeah, it is. That woman is wicked.

RICKY. Yeah, I'd hate to have to work with that bitch.

*(***KEITH** *turns on the TV. SFX: Theme for Facing Facts.)*

VICTOR. Hey! Watch your damn mouth!

(*He bops* **RICKY** *on the back of the head.*)

MIKE. Quiet! It's on.

FRANCES. (*Voice over.*) Hello, America! Welcome to tonight's edition of *Facing Facts*. I am your host, Frances Montgomery, and tonight we will be going back to the home of Ms. –

MIKE. MRS!

(*Everyone looks at* **MIKE.**)

FRANCES. (*Voice over.*) Melanie Barnsworth. You will witness her family and friends' first reaction to her amazing transformation. Ms. Barnsworth has worked extremely hard these past four weeks. She has trained with our very own fitness guru, Enrique'. She has dined on fabulous but healthy meals, prepared by the delicious Chef Louis'. Plus, she has been re-created by the ingenious make-up artist and hairstylist, Jose' De La Rosa. His beauty tips and fashion expertise are absolutely, unequivocally the best. Then, stay tuned as Joey Montego steps into the home of a family desperate to stop their son from stealing. So don't change that channel. We'll be right back with Ms. Melanie Barnsworth after these messages.

MIKE. (*He grabs the remote and angrily mutes the button.*) What happened!? Joey Montego was supposed to come here for the interview. Not that banshee from hell.

KEITH. Look on the bright side. Monica will be here.

MIKE. No offense, Keith, but that isn't my first priority. Frances Montgomery is ruthless. She tore Melanie apart. She lied about what I wrote in my letter...

(*SFX: Doorbell rings.*)

Oh my god! They're here! Quick, turn off the TV. They said to –

KEITH. I know – turn off the TV. (*He does, and then goes toward the door.*)

PAULA. Hurry! We have to stand by the door. They said to line up by the door.

(They all scurry about, bumping into each other, adlibbing 'Go'! 'Move', 'I'm there', etc. as they line up by the door.)

Ready?

MIKE. No! *(He breathes in deeply, and opens the door.)*

(**BOZ** *comes in backwards.* **FRANCES** *enters.)*

FRANCES. Here she is – the new and much improved Ms. Melanie Barnsworth!

*(***MELANIE** *steps in the doorway as* **FRANCES** *speaks.* **MIKE***'s jaw drops, as do the others.* **MELANIE** *looks fabulous.)*

Well, what do you think?

VICTOR. Son of a –

*(***PAULA** *slaps her hand over his mouth.)*

MIKE. You're beautiful, Mel….

(He hugs her. She stiffly hugs him, then crosses to **KEITH***.* **FRANCES** *notices the awkwardness.)*

KEITH. *(As he hugs* **MELANIE***.)* You look fantastic, Mom!

VICTOR. What – ya get a boob job?

*(***KEITH** *crosses to* **MONICA** *as* **VICTOR** *starts to hug* **MELANIE***.* **PAULA** *excitedly pushes him back and grabs her.* **RICKY** *comes to them.* **KEITH** *and* **MONICA** *cross behind* **BOZ***.)*

PAULA. *(She is tearing up.)* Oh, Melanie. You are fabulous!

*(***PAULA** *hugs* **MELANIE***.)*

KEITH. *(To* **MONICA***.)* What is Frances doing here?

PAULA. *(Breaking the hug.)* You look like a star! *(She hugs her again.)*

MONICA. She insisted on taking this interview.

KEITH. Why?

RICKY. You are hot, Mrs. B!

MELANIE. Oh, Ricky. *(She giggles, they hug.)* Thanks.

MONICA. I think she has a crush on your dad.

KEITH. Oh my god! She –

MONICA. Sh…

FRANCES. Isn't that something, Melanie. You even have the young stud eyeing you!

(She takes **MELANIE***, walks her to the chair and plops her in it.)*

Now, Melanie, have a seat here and we'll get right to our interview. I know the audience at home is going to want to hear all about how you achieved this fantastic makeover in only four short weeks.

(Goes to **MIKE** *and leads him to the sofa.)*

And, Mike, we'll want to hear how you have been getting along without her. You sit there on the sofa, Mike. I'll sit right next to you. Now gather around, everyone.

(She squeezes in by **MIKE***. The others stand behind the sofa. During the interview,* **FRANCES** *touches* **MIKE** *as much as possible.)*

So, Melanie, how did you enjoy staying at our beautiful, tropical resort?

MELANIE. It was unbelievable! I…

FRANCES. That's nice. And tell us – how does it feel to finally look presentable again?

MELANIE. I don't think –

FRANCES. I'm sure you don't. *(She turns to* **MIKE***.)* So, Mike, tell us how you managed to cope for these four long weeks without your little housewife?

MIKE. It was difficult.

FRANCES. I'm sure it was.

MIKE. I missed her. *(He leans toward* **MELANIE***.)* I really missed you, Melanie.

FRANCES. *(Pushing him back.)* Of course you did.

PAULA. I brought over a lot of food. He didn't go hungry.

MIKE. Yes. That's right. Paula – our neighbor – was wonderful. She's a great cook.

FRANCES. So, what did you do in the evenings to ease your loneliness? *(Insinuatingly.)* Did Paula stay with you?

MIKE. Oh, no.

VICTOR. *Hell,* no!

PAULA. Victor!

VICTOR. What? I don't like what this broad is suggesting here.

PAULA. She didn't mean…

FRANCES. Please! Let's get back to Mike. So you were lonely, Mike?

MIKE. Keith – our son – *(Points toward* **KEITH.***)*

KEITH. Hi. *(Waves awkwardly.)*

MIKE. He works in the evening, so I was by myself most of the time. It did get pretty lonely at night.

FRANCES. You poor, dear man. *(She pats his leg, keeps her hand there.)* I'm sure there's plenty of women out there in our viewing audience who would love to keep you company. I wouldn't hesitate to take a call from you anytime.

MIKE. I, uh, well, I…

MELANIE. *(Standing.)* Okay. That's enough. This interview is over.

*(***MIKE** *stands, too.)*

FRANCES. But we've just begun. The audience wants to know –

MELANIE. Stuff a sock in it!

(She turns to go toward the bedroom, but **MIKE** *gets to her, pulling her around.* **BOZ** *keeps the camera on them.)*

MIKE. Melanie –

MELANIE. Don't touch me, Mike!

MIKE. *(Still holding her arm.)* What is wrong with you, Melanie?

MELANIE. Let go of me!

MIKE. I am not letting go of you until you talk to me.

MELANIE. I have nothing to say to you!

MIKE. Well, I have plenty to say to you. I've been trying for the past four weeks to talk to you. You wouldn't answer my calls. You wouldn't give me the chance to explain.

MELANIE. You don't have to explain! Ms. Montgomery was more than happy to tell all of America how you felt!

MIKE. But she exaggerated everything I said.

MELANIE. Oh really? All right then – exactly what did you say?

MIKE. I told her how beautiful you are.

(He lets go of her arm and touches her face. She turns her head away, but doesn't move.)

MELANIE. I doubt they picked me for a makeover because of that. What else did you say?

MIKE. Well, I did say that you'd gained some weight since you had Keith.

MELANIE. Uh-huh...

MIKE. *(Overly enthusiastic.)* And that you love their resort...

MELANIE. Uh-huh...

MIKE. And uh, that, well, that you weren't exercising much...

MELANIE. That's enough, Mike. It really doesn't matter. It's obvious you don't have a clue about how I feel, or what you've put me through.

MIKE. What about how you made me feel? And what I've gone through? For the past four weeks I've been in limbo – wondering what my life was going to be like when you got home.

MELANIE. There was no need to wonder. I made it clear before I left. I want you out of here!

MIKE. And I've made it clear that I still love you!

MELANIE. You have a great way of showing it!

MIKE. What do you want me to do, Melanie? I feel like I'm trapped. No matter what I say, you turn it around. You want me to say I wish you were thinner? That I wanted you to look like the girl I married? Well, I can't do that. I don't want the girl I married. I want the woman that has grown and changed – the woman who is a better person than the one I married twenty-three years ago.

MELANIE. So – you've never wished I were thinner?

MIKE. *(Pauses.)* I won't lie to you. Sometimes I have. But never – *never* have I stopped loving you. For who you are *inside*. Unconditionally. Nothing can ever take away the love I feel for you. Not weight. Not fights. Not even *Facing Facts*. I need you, Melanie. Without you, I'm nothing.

MELANIE. *(Softening.)* And because I faced the facts – I feel like nothing. The trust we had has been shattered. And four weeks at a spa isn't long enough to put back the pieces. I just need time. I have to figure things out for myself, by myself. It will give you time to figure out what you really want, too.

MIKE. I know what I want. *(Steps toward couch.)* You think I'd be chasing you around the couch if I didn't still want you?

MELANIE. Yes. You're horny. All men are horny.

MIKE. That's not true. Well, yes it is. But that has nothing to do with it. You should be glad I still want you.

*(***MELANIE***, ***PAULA***, ***KEITH***, and ***MONICA*** *gasp.)*

RICKY. Dude!

MIKE. *(***MELANIE*** *turns toward the bedroom.* ***MIKE*** *tries to stop her.)* Wait, Melanie. *(He turns her toward him.)* That didn't come out right…Melanie…please, I – Melanie

*(***MELANIE*** *pulls away, He grabs her arm again, and she pushes him off balance. He falls onto* ***FRANCES****' lap.* ***MELANIE*** *rushes out to bedroom.)*

MIKE. Melanie! *(He tries to get up, but* ***FRANCES*** *restrains him.)*

FRANCES. That, my friends, is good television. We'll be back in a moment. *(Camera goes down. Her arms are around* **MIKE**.*)*

KEITH. Dad…*(Starts to help him up.)*

FRANCES. Stay in your place. I have everything under control.

*(***KEITH*** stops.)*

Monica! Bring me a towel.

*(***MONICA*** crosses to her with towel;* **FRANCES** *wipes* **MIKE***'s brow and cradles him to her as the others gawk.)*

You poor man. Are you all right? My goodness, your wife is a spitfire. How in the world do you put up with her?

MIKE. It's my fault, I…

FRANCES. Don't be absurd, you precious man. You have done nothing to her. She's just being ungrateful. And after all I've – the *show* – has done for her.

BOZ. We're back in 10 seconds…

PAULA. Mike, can I do –*(Starts to move to* **MIKE**.*)*

FRANCES. Move back. We're almost on again. You'll be in the way.

*(***PAULA*** goes back behind the sofa.)*

BOZ. And five, four, three, two…*(Silent 'one',* **BOZ** *points at* **FRANCES**.*)*

FRANCES. And we're back ladies and gentlemen, with dear, misunderstood Mike Barnsworth. His ungrateful wife, Melanie, has just assaulted him. I hope you didn't miss it!

(She finally lets **MIKE** *go, and he sits up straight with his back to the archway.* **MELANIE** *enters with his suitcase.)*

Mike, tell us – how do you put up with her spiteful vindictiveness?

MIKE. She usually isn't like this. She's upset with me.

FRANCES. Upset about what? That you cared enough to send her away to a fantastic tropical resort?

(MIKE absently nods after each question.)

Upset that she was totally pampered by an international staff of experts? Upset that she was changed from a dowdy housewife to a *decent* looking woman?

(FRANCES manipulates his face, making him nod closer to her.)

MELANIE. How nice of you to agree, Mike. It makes it that much easier to throw you out! *(She throws his suitcase down.)*

MIKE. Agree with what?

MELANIE. With that! *(She points at FRANCES.)*

MIKE. *(Standing.)* Now, Melanie, sweetheart, you need to calm down.

MELANIE. Oh, I am calm. And the sooner you, Ms. Montgomery, and her crew get out of my house, the calmer I'll be. You can go sit in her lap and let her nurse your fragile ego!

MIKE. That's crazy, Melanie. You aren't making sense. My ego has nothing to do with this.

MELANIE. Now I'm insane, too?

MIKE. I didn't say that!

MELANIE. It sounded like it to me.

MIKE. You are being unreasonable, Melanie.

MELANIE. Fat, insane and unreasonable. Anything else you'd like to add to my resume?

FRANCES. *(Standing, she pushes MIKE aside and crosses to MELANIE.)* I can! Ungrateful, hateful, and common!

MELANIE. That's it. I've taken too much from you! I am sick of your continuous insults. A belly the size of Georgia, chunky little housewife that ballooned out of control, Mellie's belly isn't from baby fat! Common!!

FRANCES. The truth hurts when you have to face the facts!

MELANIE. *(She starts advancing on FRANCES, who backs away. As she speaks, the action slowly passes the sofa, to dining room table, then around, behind table, then finally in front of*

table. **BOZ** *walks backwards to catch it all on camera.*)
Well, here are some facts *you* can face…

FRANCES. It looks like that's all the time we…

(**FRANCES** *tries to signal* **BOZ** *to stop filming, by 'slashing' at her throat, etc.* **BOZ** *ignores her and keeps on filming.*)

MELANIE (*Over* **FRANCES**.) You are a conniving witch who doesn't care what she does to others. You manipulate people! You don't want to help them. You want to *humiliate* them for the sake of a few ratings points. You take average, happy people, and make them feel like they aren't good enough to even exist. Not everyone wants to look like an emaciated mannequin with a plastic face. (**MELANIE** *sees the dip on the table.*) How about something to soften those wrinkles even more? (*She takes a handful of dip and smears it into* **FRANCES'** *face, then turns to the camera.*) And now for a word from our sponsor. (**MELANIE** *wipes her hands on a wet one or napkin.*)

BOZ. (*Bringing the camera down.*) Now *that* is *great* television!

FRANCES. *MONICA!* Get this stuff off of me! (*She runs toward* **MONICA**, **RICKY** *stops her.*)

RICKY. (*He takes a finger full of dip from* **FRANCES'** *face and licks it.*) It's better on a chip.

FRANCES. Oh! Cretin! (*She slaps at* **RICKY**, *and he ducks out of the way.*)

MONICA. Here, Ms. Montgomery, let me… (*She starts wiping* **FRANCES'** *face, trying not to laugh.*)

FRANCES. (*Grabs towel from* **MONICA** *and pushes her away.*)
Oh, get away! (*Turns to* **MELANIE**.) You will be hearing from my lawyer.

MELANIE. Fine! It should bring you lots of juicy publicity.

FRANCES. (*Frustrated.*) Oh! (*Looks towards* **BOZ**.) Boz! Why are you standing there? Get me out of here! (*She turns and crosses to door, growls at* **RICKY**. *Turns to* **MONICA**.) Monica! (**FRANCES** *waits for* **MONICA** *to open the door, finally does it herself, and storms out.*)

BOZ. *(To* **MELANIE.***)* Thanks, Lady. You made my day. Hell, you made my year!

*(***BOZ** *and* **MONICA** *follow* **FRANCES** *out.* **MONICA** *waves toward* **KEITH**, *who waves back.)*

MELANIE. *(Pulling herself together.)* Well. *(Turns to the others.)* Thank you all for being here to witness part two of The Humiliation of Melanie Barnsworth. I do hope you've enjoyed the show. And now…*(She starts crossing towards the arch.)* I am going into my room, turn out the lights, and crawl into my bed. *(She is by* **MIKE**.*)* When I feel fairly certain I can come out of my room and face the world again, I will call you.

MIKE. Melanie, you –

MELANIE. *(She holds up her hand.)* At that time, Mike, you may come collect the rest of your things. *(She turns and goes into the bedroom and slams the door.)*

MIKE. *(Pause.)* I guess that's that. *(He picks up his suitcase, crosses to the door, and turns to* **KEITH**.*)* I'll see you soon, Keith. *(They hug.)*

KEITH. Don't give up hope, Dad. I'll talk to her.

VICTOR. Yeah. I will too. *(Everyone looks at him.)* What?

MIKE. Thanks, but I think she just needs to be alone for a while – to think. And all I can hope for is a miracle.

(He turns and walks out the door.)

(Lights out.)

Scene 2

(It's the following Saturday, late afternoon. The doorbell rings. **KEITH** *comes from the bedroom to answer it.)*

KEITH. *(As he opens the door.)* Dad! Why'd you ring the bell?

MIKE. Hi, son. It's good to see you, too.

KEITH. *(Hugging* **MIKE.***)* Sorry. Hi, Dad. How are you?

MIKE. I'm doing all right. Is your mom here?

KEITH. No. *(They cross to sit.)* She's shopping. She wanted to be out of the house when...

MIKE. It's okay. I know she didn't want to see me. That's why I rang. In case she was here, I didn't want to just barge in like I live here.

KEITH. That sounds really strange.

MIKE. Yeah, it does.

KEITH. How's the apartment?

MIKE. It's every guy's dream.

KEITH. Really?

MIKE. Yeah. A nightmare. You'll have to come over soon.

KEITH. How about right now? You busy?

MIKE. After I finish getting my things, I have a hot date with Meryl Streep.

KEITH. Meryl Streep?

MIKE. Yeah. I rented Kramer vs. Kramer.

KEITH. Why would you want to punish yourself like that?

MIKE. It's a great movie.

KEITH. But not one you need to see right now. No. You're not going home to watch that. Instead, I'm taking you bowling. You can take out some of your frustrations on the pins.

MIKE. I can't, Keith. I have to get my things.

KEITH. That can wait. Besides, if you don't get them now, maybe you won't ever have to.

MIKE. Don't count on it, son. Your mom is pretty strong headed when she's hurt.

KEITH. She's also sensible. Usually.

MIKE. I don't know, Keith. She'll get mad if I don't clear my things out.

KEITH. No she won't. I'll tell her I wanted to spend some time with you. I'm taking her to dinner tonight, so she'll understand.

MIKE. Well…why not?

KEITH. Good!

MIKE. *(Standing.)* We better leave before she gets back.

KEITH. Hold on. I gotta get my cell phone so I can call Monica. *(Runs to his room.)*

MIKE. So, you and Monica are getting close, huh?

KEITH. *(Entering.)* Yeah, she's great. Dad…I think I may have found my soul mate.

MIKE. Wow! It's that serious?

KEITH. I think so.

MIKE. How does your mom feel about that?

KEITH. She doesn't know yet. But she will soon. I'm bringing Monica to dinner with Mom and me tonight.

MIKE. Do you think that's a good idea…so soon after Monday's show?

KEITH. It's time. Monica and I have been dating for almost five weeks now. I want Mom to get to know her.

MIKE. I know you do. Just be prepared for a little resistance. The people involved with *Facing Facts* probably aren't at the top of your mom's best buddies list.

KEITH. Monica isn't Frances Montgomery.

MIKE. That's true, but she's connected to her.

KEITH. Well, she's nothing like her.

MIKE. You know who Monica reminds me of?

KEITH. Who?

MIKE. Your mom.

KEITH. Really?

MIKE. Yeah – back in our college days. Sweet, innocent, mischievous – and a little off the wall.

KEITH. I can see that.

MIKE. *(Pauses.)* What if she never takes me back? She's *my* soul mate. What would I do?

KEITH. Don't think like that, Dad. Stay positive and –

MIKE. I know…give it time. Speaking of which, if we don't get going, you'll have to be back before we ever leave.

(They cross to the door.)

KEITH. Prepare to be stomped. Basketball may be your court, but I rule the lanes.

MIKE. Don't count your pins before they fall, boy!

(They exit.)

(Lights out.)

Scene 3

*(Two hours later. Keys rattle, the door opens, and **MELANIE** enters with several shopping bags, including one from Soma's Lingerie. She crosses to sofa putting the bags down. She crosses into the kitchen humming, and returns with the cordless phone and yellow pages. She sits at table and flips through the book.)*

MELANIE. AA Auto…AAA Auto…Auto One? …What's the name of that place?

*(SFX: Doorbell. The door opens. It's **PAULA**.)*

Come in. It's open.

PAULA. I've been waiting for you all afternoon. Where have – *(Sees "Attorney" in Yellow Pages, swings book around to look.)* Are you looking for a divorce attorney?

MELANIE. No! I'm trying to find the number for the auto shop Mike always takes the car to. It's making a weird whiny noise.

PAULA. Oh. So where have you been?

MELANIE. I decided it was time to face the world again, so I went shopping. It was crazy. People actually recognized me from the show.

PAULA. They did?

MELANIE. Yeah. I was so afraid to face the public, but they loved me. People smiled and waved. Some just stared, like they weren't sure where they'd seen me before. I even got a high-five from one of the salesgirls. It was awesome!

PAULA. I bet. It looks like you bought out the mall.

MELANIE. Just about. Everything in my closet is too big. Well, except for a few things that I couldn't wear before. But a new body needs new styles. I think I hit every store!

PAULA. No wonder it took you so long.

MELANIE. Well, I wanted to be out of the house when Mike came to get his things.

PAULA. Still not ready to talk to him?

MELANIE. No.

PAULA. Okay. Ooo – What's in the lingerie bag?

MELANIE. *(Pulling out a push up bra.)* The latest in push up bras. You don't think these puppies are sitting up here on their own, do you?

PAULA. I need to get one of those! Victor would think he had died and gone to heaven. On second thought, my sports bra is just fine...

MELANIE. You know, I haven't shopped for clothes much the last few years – it was too depressing. It felt so good buying clothes that were two sizes smaller. And I never bought bras like this before. It's a new world.

PAULA. You loved it, huh?

MELANIE. At first. But then I started to get upset.

PAULA. Why?

MELANIE. Exactly! Why should a size 12 have ten times the clothing options? Why can't bigger women have the same choices – and more choices? Why do so many of the really cute clothes only go up to size 16? And who designs for plus sizes? Most of the clothes over size 16 are designed for women over eighty! I'll admit that it's much better than it used to be. A few years ago all you could find were stretch pants and oversized blouses. Or mumus. And in the department stores – who had the brilliant idea to put the plus sizes in the back corner of the store? Like they're embarrassed to even have them. You have to walk past the more stylish clothes – made only for tiny butts – to get to the 'women's world'. And worst of all, half the time plus sizes are right next to petites! Petites! But the *prices* are *higher*! *(She turns to* **PAULA.**) I'm ranting, aren't I?

PAULA. A little bit. Why are you so angry, Melanie?

MELANIE. Because of the injustice! In our country people are bigger now than ever before. I'm not saying it's good – I know it's a major health crisis. But I didn't wake up one morning and say, 'you know, I think I want to get fat!' It just happened, and it's happening to more and more people. Even so, the overweight club is bombarded with negativity.

PAULA. How do you mean?

MELANIE. For instance, are there any role models out there for young girls that aren't stick thin? No! Look at the models and actresses of today... *(She picks up a magazine from the coffee table.)* Not only are most of them emaciated, their pictures are airbrushed into perfection! The rare one that has a little meat on her bones – the media tears her apart! Not everyone was born to be a size six! Even in commercials – are the women ever overweight? Maybe one in a hundred. But only if she's funny! It's just not fair! *(She sits.)*

PAULA. Who said anything in life is fair?

MELANIE. You're skinny. You have no idea what it's like.

PAULA. I may not have a weight problem, but I've got my share.

MELANIE. Everyone has problems, Paula. But weight is an issue that is above and beyond. It's like people expect you to be perfect, because being fat is fault enough.

PAULA. But you've lost so much weight. You're looking great.

MELANIE. Thanks. I don't feel it. I look in the mirror and I see a body that's in better shape, but in my soul...I still feel critical eyes glaring back at me. I hear...in my mind...I hear people thinking, "Wow, she really let herself go," or "But she has such a pretty face," or "I wonder why that hunk is with *her*"...

PAULA. I had no idea you felt this way, Melanie. Do you really think people are that vicious?

MELANIE. You hear it on TV all the time. Like in sitcoms... lying is okay, cheating is okay...manipulating is mandatory! But be overweight? The insults start flying.

PAULA. You're right. I have noticed that.

MELANIE. It's the last acceptable prejudice.

PAULA. Well, it's not acceptable. But it's not your problem

anymore, either.

MELANIE. It will always be my problem, Paula. It will remain a constant battle to get thin. And stay there.

PAULA. You're well on your way, Melanie.

MELANIE. You think so?

PAULA. Yes!

MELANIE. You want to know a secret?

PAULA. Of course I do.

MELANIE. *(Crosses to sofa, moves bags and sits by* **PAULA.***)* You think I look great. Right?

PAULA. You look fabulous.

MELANIE. It's a mirage.

PAULA. What do you mean a mirage?

MELANIE. Paula, I only lost thirteen pounds while I was away.

PAULA. No way! You look like you lost thirty.

MELANIE. I know. Now, I did exercise. That helped me tone up, and it added some muscle weight. But I have only lost a fraction of what I need to lose. So basically, it's a mirage.

PAULA. I can't believe it.

MELANIE. They changed my make-up, my hairstyle, and my clothes. They taught me how to make myself look – sleeker.

PAULA. But you did lose thirteen pounds, and you're exercising now.

MELANIE. Oh, I know I look better, and I intend to keep it up. But I'm going to battle the weight issue for the rest of my life.

PAULA. Well, you know I love you no matter what...so does Mike.

MELANIE. Please, Paula.

PAULA. You're going to have to face him some time, Melanie. The sooner, the better.

MELANIE. The *later*, the better. I'm just not ready yet.

PAULA. *(Overlapping* **MELANIE**.*)*…ready yet. Just don't wait until it's too late, Melanie. *(She pats* **MELANIE***'s hand and rises.)* Speaking of late, I better get home and start dinner.

MELANIE. Before you go, tell me…which blouse should I wear tonight? Keith and I have a date – we're going to dinner.

PAULA. He's not working tonight?

MELANIE. No. He took the night off so he could take his mother out. *(Holds up a blouse from a bag.)* How do you like this one?

PAULA. That's pretty. I like it.

MELANIE. Okay. How about this one? *(Holds up another blouse.)*

PAULA. Ooo, I really like that one. It fits the new you!

MELANIE. Thanks. *(Hugs* **PAULA**.*)* And thanks for listening.

PAULA. Listening is good. You should try it sometime…

MELANIE. *(Turns* **PAULA** *towards the front door, and pops her bottom.)* Okay, you, out!

PAULA. Ouch! You're getting feisty! Have fun with Keith. *(As she exits.)*

MELANIE. I will!

(She gathers up bags and exits into bedroom, humming. After a beat, **KEITH** *and* **MONICA** *enter the house.)*

KEITH. Mom? I'm home! *(He sees yellow pages open. Looks at it.* **MONICA** *sets purse down.)* Oh my god!*(He quickly shuts book, not wanting* **MONICA** *to see.)*

MONICA. What?

MELANIE. *(Offstage.)* I'll be out in a minute.

KEITH. Nothing.

MONICA. Are you sure this is a good idea, Keith? Surprising your mom like this?

KEITH. Why not? I want her to meet you.

MONICA. She already has, if you'll remember. It was a disaster.

KEITH. She needs to meet you away from the show. So she can get to know you.

MONICA. I'm so nervous. What if she hates me?

KEITH. She has to love you. I do!

MONICA. *(Smiling.)* You do?

KEITH. Yeah. I do.

(They kiss as MELANIE walks out.)

MELANIE. OH! Sorry...

(Flustered, she turns towards the hall, stops, realizes what she saw, and swings back around. KEITH and MONICA face MELANIE.)

YOU!

KEITH. Mom, this is Monica. Monica, Melanie.

MONICA. Hello, Mrs. – *(Steps toward MELANIE, but stops.)*

MELANIE. *(Points at MONICA.)* You! *(Points to KEITH.)* And you! *(To MONICA.)* With...you! *(To KEITH.)* How could you?

KEITH. Mom, Monica and I have been dating for quite awhile.

MELANIE. *(Shakes her finger around.)* You have got to be kidding me.

KEITH. No, I'm serious. *We're* serious. In fact, I love her.

MELANIE. Love her? How could you love her after what she did to me?

KEITH. *She* didn't do anything to you, Mom.

MELANIE. She was a part of it. She works for that she-devil who ruined my life!

KEITH. It's just her job.

MONICA. It's just my job.

MELANIE. It's just your job to help that woman destroy people?

KEITH. MOM!

MELANIE. What, Keith? Didn't we teach you the concept of guilt by association?

KEITH. This is different. It's not vandalism or...or drugs. It's her job, and Monica can't control what happens on *Facing Facts*. Besides, she is nothing like Frances Montgomery.

MONICA. I don't even like her. It's just a summer internship.

MELANIE. *(Pause.)* I see. I'm sorry. The whole thing is still a little fresh for me right now. You two go on without me. If you will excuse me...*(She turns to go back to the bedroom.)*

KEITH. No, Mom. You aren't excused. *(***MELANIE** *turns to him incredulously.)* You need to get to know Monica. Come out with us.

MELANIE. I'm sorry Keith. I'm just not up to it now.

KEITH. You know, Mom, everything isn't about you.

MELANIE. I never said it was!

KEITH. Well, you're acting like it is! *(Pauses, steps toward* **MELANIE.***)* Look, I know you were hurt. But if you'd stop obsessing about *your* feelings, and think about mine – and Dad's, maybe you could finally get over it. *(Pause. He turns to* **MONICA.***)* Come on, let's go. *(He guides* **MONICA** *to the door. He turns back to* **MELANIE.***)* If...no, *when* you get to know Monica, I think you'll like her, Mom. And stop looking in the yellow pages! *(They exit.)*

MELANIE. *(Crosses to the sofa and sits, looks at the sleeve of her blouse, and pulls on it. Sighs.)* The new me. I wonder who that is. *(Pause.)* What's wrong with the yellow pages?

(Lights out.)

Scene 4

(Sunday afternoon. The doorbell rings erratically, several times. The door opens, and **RICKY** *slides in 'Kramer style' holding a tennis bag.)*

RICKY. Hey Keith! You ready?

KEITH *(Offstage.)* Yeah, I'll be right there.

RICKY. Hurry up. We only have the court for an hour. *(He begins extensive stretching which continues for several lines, dipping behind the sofa at times, unseen.)*

KEITH. *(Entering.)* We've got plenty of time. (**KEITH** *crosses to paper on table.)* Hold on. I'm gonna leave Mom a note.

RICKY. Aw, will she worry about where her little boy is?

KEITH. Knock it off. I'm just letting her know…it's been tense enough around here.

RICKY. Oh, yeah?

KEITH. Yeah. I brought Monica over last night to go to dinner with Mom and me –

RICKY. Eeww. Not good, huh?

KEITH. Not at all. Mom wasn't too thrilled about me dating Frances Montgomery's assistant.

RICKY. I bet she wasn't. Got nasty, huh?

KEITH. Yeah. Mom's got a pretty wicked streak herself.

RICKY. What happened?

KEITH. Let's just say I won't be bringing Monica around for a while…not until Mom quits freaking out about this whole thing.

RICKY. Freak outs aside, you gotta be proud of your mom. I mean, she's really been working on it, man.

KEITH. Yeah, she is looking good!

RICKY. She isn't just looking good. She's getting hot!

KEITH. Are you *sick*? That's my mom you're talking about. She's like your aunt or something.

RICKY. What's the big deal? I was just saying –

KEITH. You know what? I don't want to play tennis anymore.

In fact, I think you better leave... *(Starts pushing **RICKY** towards the door.)*

RICKY. *(Circling back to **KEITH**.)* Chill out, Keith. It's not like I want to have sex with her. I just...

KEITH. Oh my god! You and my mom.... *(Starts pushing **RICKY** around behind the table.)*

RICKY. I didn't say...

KEITH. You didn't have to. First Ms. Joyce, now my mother!

*(He pushes **RICKY** in front of the table, gets him in a headlock; **RICKY** twists **KEITH** around and pulls him to the floor, face down. **RICKY** sits on **KEITH**, pulling a leg up so that **KEITH** can't move.)*

AGH!

RICKY. AGH! *(**KEITH** squirms, **RICKY** holds him down.)* You give? I'm not letting you up until you chill out. *(**KEITH** squirms again; **RICKY** holds his face down.)* Can you talk rationally?

*(**KEITH** is finally still.)*

KEITH. Yes!

RICKY. Are you sure?

KEITH. Yes! Get off of me. *(**RICKY** lets him up.)* Where the hell did you learn that?

RICKY. Ms. Joyce. *(Crosses to sofa and sits, **KEITH** follows.)* Listen, man, I'm sorry. I wasn't trying to upset you.

KEITH. No. It's my fault. I've been kinda on edge since all this started.

RICKY. Yeah, I can see that.

KEITH. It's just...Mom runs around here like she's never been happier. She won't talk to Dad. She's irrational about Monica...

RICKY. It's all new to her, Keith. She'll come around.

KEITH. Yeah, in the meantime, it's driving me nuts. And I can't stand what this separation is doing to Dad.

RICKY. Are they getting counseling?

KEITH. No. She was even looking in the yellow pages for a lawyer yesterday.

RICKY. I didn't know it had gone that far. Jeez, I always thought it would be my parents. Not yours.

KEITH. I still think there's hope…that they'll work it out. I can't imagine them actually divorcing.

RICKY. Yeah. That would suck.

(The front door opens and MELANIE and PAULA enter with their hands full of grocery bags. The boys don't react to them. PAULA crosses to put a bag she is carrying for MELANIE on the table.)

PAULA. Oh, that's all right. No need to greet us. We'll just handle all these bags ourselves.

(The boys turn, see their mothers, and jump up to help them.)

KEITH. *(Taking bags from MELANIE.)* Here.

MELANIE. Thanks. Those go in the kitchen.

KEITH. You mean there is food in the grocery bags?

MELANIE. Yes. That's usually what's in them.

KEITH. *(Crossing to kitchen.)* Sorry, but things haven't been 'as usual' around here, have they? *(He exits.)*

MELANIE. Are you boys going to play tennis today, Ricky?

RICKY. Uh, we were, but I think we're going to cancel.

MELANIE. Oh? Why?

RICKY. I don't know…Keith's just a…a little fried, I guess.

MELANIE. Fried?

RICKY. Yeah, you know. Upset. About things. You know.

MELANIE. Oh. Thanks, Ricky.

RICKY. No prob.

PAULA. Can you take the bags home, Ricky? I'll be there in a minute.

RICKY. Sure, Mom. *(Gets tennis bag.)* Bye, Mrs. B.

MELANIE. *(Deep in thought.)* Bye…

PAULA. Melanie?

MELANIE. Yes? *(Looks at PAULA.)* What?

PAULA. I don't know how to say this, exactly…

MELANIE. Just say it.

PAULA. I think…do *you* think…do you think you're being fair to Mike?

MELANIE. How can you ask that, Paula? After what he did to me?

PAULA. Until you talk to him again –

MELANIE. I have nothing left to say to him.

PAULA. Yes, you do, Melanie. And he has so much to say to you.

MELANIE. Don't you think we said enough to each other the night I came back home?

PAULA. No. That night you both spoke in anger – or frustration. You need to sit down and talk to each other. Really talk. And listen…

MELANIE. What great advice, Paula. I tell you what, when you and Victor can get through one evening together without verbally assaulting each other, maybe I'll listen. Until then, please keep your second-rate marriage counseling to yourself. Maybe it would do you some good. *(She turns away from* **PAULA.***)*

PAULA. *(Pauses, walks toward front door.)* You know, Melanie, if you can stop feeling sorry for yourself long enough to see that you are alienating everyone who loves you, maybe then your makeover will be complete. *(Exits.)*

MELANIE. *(Turns toward* **PAULA,** *just as the door shuts.)* Paula, I'm…I'm such a bitch.

KEITH. *(Entering from kitchen.)* Mom?

MELANIE. What? Oh, Keith. You startled me.

KEITH. Sorry. *(Pause.)* Did you and Paula…have a fight?

MELANIE. No. It was all me. I behaved like a raving lunatic.

KEITH. That sounds familiar.

MELANIE. It does?

KEITH. Yeah. I attacked my best friend today, too.

MELANIE. Oh. Why?

KEITH. Probably for the same reason you did…Mom, don't you think it's about time all this stopped?

MELANIE. Yes. But it's not that easy.

KEITH. Why not? I mean, don't you still love Dad?

MELANIE. Of course I do. It's just…he's never hurt me like this before.

KEITH. Do you honestly think Dad would hurt you on purpose?

MELANIE. I…No.

KEITH. Then talk to him. Give him a call.

MELANIE. I don't know if I'm ready yet, Keith.

KEITH. What are you waiting for?

MELANIE. …An epiphany?

KEITH. I hope it comes to you…soon. *(He gives her a hug and kisses her cheek.)* I love you, Mom.

MELANIE. I love you, too, Keith. And listen, I'm sorry about last night…with Monica. I'm sure she's a very nice girl.

KEITH. She is Mom. She's great. *(He looks at his watch.)* She said she was going to Jerry's Bar tonight. I think I'll see if I can catch her there.

MELANIE. Okay. Have fun. And be careful.

KEITH. I will. *(Starts to cross to door and stops.)* Mom…

MELANIE. Yes?

KEITH. Dad's cell phone is always on. Think about it.*(He exits.)*

*(***MELANIE*** looks around her empty house, and crosses to the kitchen. She comes back in with the phone, crosses to the sofa. She looks at the phone for a moment, and then dials.)*

MELANIE. …Hello, Victor. Is Paula there?…She did? That's nice of her – she's a great cook…Mike will appreciate it. Uh, will you leave her a note for me?…No, write it down. You men never remember to tell us to call each other back…You're right, he's not. Listen, just tell her I'd like to see her when she gets back. The door is open…Thanks…

(She sets the phone on the table, looks around and sighs. She picks up the phone, puts it down. She looks at her wedding ring.)

What are you afraid of? Dial the number!

*(She picks up the phone and starts to dial, and the doorbell rings. She puts the phone down, gets up and crosses to the door, and opens it. It's **VICTOR**.)*

Victor! What are you doing here?

VICTOR. You sounded lonely. I thought I'd come over and cheer you up.

MELANIE. That's nice, but you didn't…

VICTOR. *(Comes in the door and shuts it.)* Nonsense. What are friends for? Paula is over at Mike's apartment, cheering him up, so I thought I'd come over and do the same for you.

(He goes to hug her; she gives him a short hug and walks past him.)

MELANIE. I'm fine. Really. Besides, Keith is due back here any minute.

VICTOR. That's funny. I just saw him leaving. He got a date tonight? With that sassy little redhead from the show? What's her name? Monique?

MELANIE. Monica.

VICTOR. Yeah, Monica. He's not going to see her?

MELANIE. Yes, but…I'm, uh…

VICTOR. *You* are looking so damn good since you got that makeover. You aren't as fluffy anymore.

(He approaches her again. She moves away.)

MELANIE. As I was saying, I'm really not feeling well, Victor. I was thinking I'd take a hot bath and go to bed early.

VICTOR. Sounds good to me. *(Playfully.)* How 'bout I scrub that beautiful back for you?

(He approaches her and she walks away.)

MELANIE. I…I…*(She suddenly stops and turns to him.)* I think that sounds like a marvy idea.

VICTOR. You do?

(**VICTOR** *begins backing up as* **MELANIE** *approaches.*)

MELANIE. *(She starts pawing at him and mussing his hair.)* In fact, maybe you'd like to join me in a hot, foamy, bubble bath. After all, Mike is gone, Keith's not here, Paula's not home...

(**MELANIE** *puts her arms around him. He is trying to take them off, and she keeps putting them back.*)

VICTOR. I, uh, well, I was just stopping by for a second...I gotta...

MELANIE. Come on now, Victor...aren't you – up to it?

VICTOR. Listen, Melanie, I better head home. It's getting late.

MELANIE. It's never too late for a little neighborly one-on-one.

(*She grabs his butt cheeks. He yelps and jumps away, moves toward the door, gets it cracked open, but she stops him from leaving. She paws at him as he walks backward toward the right arm of the sofa.*)

What's the matter, Victor? You aren't feeling uncomfortable, are you? *Are you?*

VICTOR. *(At second 'Are you?' he falls over the arm of the sofa.)* Come on, Melanie. You don't...*(He tries to get off the sofa.)*

MELANIE. Don't you move a muscle.

(*He stops and stares at her.*)

How do you like it, Victor?

VICTOR. Wha...

MELANIE. How do you like being harassed?

VICTOR. I –

MELANIE. Victor, I am sick and tired of you harassing me every time I see you!

VICTOR. I never...

MELANIE. You always! Do you have any idea how it makes

me feel when you constantly make lewd passes at me, or make comments about my weight?

VICTOR. It's harmless fun –

MELANIE. No. It's *not* fun! In the past, when I was – 'fluffier', as you call it, I barely acknowledged your 'harmless' harassment. It seemed…ineffective. But now, I find it insulting. No, I always found it insulting, but I never had the guts to confront you. My lack of self-esteem allowed you to continue your belligerent behavior towards me. But I'm not going to put up with your crap anymore. Now I realize the big ass – is you!

VICTOR. *(He tries to get up from the sofa. She pushes him back down.)* Hey, calm down, I was just…

(PAULA opens the front door slightly. They don't notice her.)

MELANIE. You weren't just anything! God, I feel sorry for Paula. Does she realize what a jerk you can be?

VICTOR. *(He starts to sit up on the sofa again. This time she lets him.)* I…well, I – what do I say to that? That's one of those redundant questions.

MELANIE. Oh, is it? I think you mean rhetorical. But redundant applies as well, considering it's so obvious.

VICTOR. Listen, let's forget about it. No foul, huh?

MELANIE. Yes, it is foul, Victor. Foul and disgusting.

VICTOR. I…uh, I didn't know what I was…

MELANIE. Yes, you did. You knew exactly what you were doing. You have always treated me inappropriately. A little slap and tickle wouldn't hurt. Not with the big broad.

VICTOR. Hey, calm down. You aren't as big…

MELANIE. That's hardly the point, Victor. Your behavior is the point. You can be a nice guy. He's just hard to find sometimes. And Victor, I think you should come clean. You should tell Paula how you've been behaving.

VICTOR. Why the hell would I do that?

MELANIE. Because she has the right to know. If you don't tell her, I will.

VICTOR. But, what'll I tell her?

PAULA. Don't worry. I've already heard it.

(**MELANIE** and **VICTOR** are in shock. **VICTOR** jumps up.)

MELANIE. I'm so sorry, Paula. I didn't hear you come in.

VICTOR. I can explain, honey…

PAULA. Save it, Victor. Can we have a minute, Melanie?

MELANIE. Sure. I'll be in here. (She exits into her bedroom.)

VICTOR. (Goes to look around corner at archway, then whispers to **PAULA**.) Listen, Paula. She's gone wacko. Ever since she got back, she …

PAULA. Stop, Victor.

VICTOR. But I…

PAULA. Do you think I'm a complete moron, Victor?

VICTOR. Of course not, honey. You're not a moron at all.

PAULA. That's right. I'm not. You are.

VICTOR. Now, listen…

PAULA. No. You are going to listen to me. From now on, this is how it's going to be. Victor…I have put up with your crap for over two decades. Some people would think I'm crazy. I'm not. Not technically. I think I'm an optimist. I tend to think the best of people, and that people can learn to be their best. Well, I'm tired, Victor. I'm tired of waiting for you to want to be your best.

VICTOR. Hey, there's nothing wrong with me.

PAULA. No, there isn't. There isn't anything wrong with you that a year or two of therapy and Prozac won't help.

VICTOR. Now wait a minute. I'm not depressed. And I don't need a damn shrink!

PAULA. I think you do, Victor. There's nothing wrong with getting help when you need it.

VICTOR. Who the hell are you to tell me what I need?

PAULA. Your wife, who loves you. And it's about time I told you the truth. I have enabled you all this time. I've been in denial, and you are up to your neck in denial.

VICTOR. I'm in denial? About what?

PAULA. About your childhood. About our family…You always said you wanted more kids –

VICTOR. And you wouldn't have them.

PAULA. I never felt that we were stable enough to bring more children into our home. What we needed was help – to keep our family together. And now, if you want to stay together, you're going to have to take the next step.

VICTOR. I don't know…I…Maybe it's too late.

PAULA. It's never to late to get better. So, what will it be? Will you try to get better?

(He nods. She kisses him softly.)

Good. You can start now.

VICTOR. Now?

PAULA. Yes. You owe our friend an apology, don't you think?

VICTOR. Yeah. *(He shouts towards the bedroom.)* Hey! Melanie!

PAULA. Victor!

VICTOR. Oh, right. Uh, Melanie, can you please come back out?

MELANIE. *(Coming back in.)* Yes, Victor?

VICTOR. Uh, about the uh, the fluffy stuff…

MELANIE. Yes?

VICTOR. And the, uh…you know, the…other stuff…

MELANIE. Yes?

VICTOR. Uh, no foul, huh?

PAULA. Victor…

VICTOR. Okay…I'm sorry – huh?

MELANIE. Apology accepted.

VICTOR. So, we're okay, then?

MELANIE. We'll be okay. Listen, I have a great pot roast in the fridge. A fabulous cook brought it to me. You two want to stay for dinner?

PAULA. Thanks, but we better get home. We have a lot to talk about.

(**PAULA** *and* **VICTOR** *start crossing to the door.*)

MELANIE. Okay, but you don't know what you're missing.

PAULA. *(Stopping,* **VICTOR** *goes through the door.)* Melanie, you *do* know what you're missing. Maybe it's time for you to talk, too.

MELANIE. I love you, Paula.

PAULA. You too.

(She exits.)

(**MELANIE** *shuts the door. She walks to the coffee table and picks up the phone and begins to dial as the lights go out.*)

Scene 5

(Later that night. Lights up as **MELANIE** *is looking out the window. She crosses to table and checks make-up in compact, doorbell rings. She puts compact in purse, and purse in chair, then crosses and opens the door.* **MIKE** *enters, holding flowers.)*

MELANIE. Oh, how beautiful. You didn't have to…Thank you.

MIKE. You're welcome.

MELANIE. I – I'll need to put them in water. I'll go get a vase. *(She starts toward the kitchen.)* Go ahead and sit. I'll be right back.

MIKE. Okay. I'll – sit.

(She exits to kitchen. He crosses to sofa and sits, trying to look relaxed, gets up, crosses to chair, sits more rigidly. Gets up. Starts to sit on the sofa as **MELANIE** *comes back in, he rises again and stands between sofa and chair.)*

MELANIE. *(Puts flowers on table, crosses to sit on sofa, patting sofa.)* Sit here, Mike.

MIKE. *(***MIKE** *sits on sofa. Pause.)* So, how have you been? Well?

MELANIE. Yes. And you?

MIKE. Just great. No, not great. But – well.

MELANIE. Good. That's good. *(Pause.)* Would you like a glass of wine? Or a beer?

MIKE. No, thanks. But thank you.

MELANIE. Scotch? Bourbon?

MIKE. No. Thanks.

MELANIE. Gin and tonic?

MIKE. That's okay. Thanks.

MELANIE. Okay. *(Pause.)*

MIKE. I, uh, I was glad you called.

MELANIE. Yeah.

MIKE. I was hoping you would.

MELANIE. Yeah.

MIKE. Melanie, I –*(He suddenly turns to her and takes her hands.)* I've missed you so much.

MELANIE. I've missed you, too.

MIKE. I have so much I want to say to you. I want you to understand why I did – what I did.

MELANIE. Mike, I know why you did it.

MIKE. No, you don't. You only know what Frances Montgomery said. And she lied. She exaggerated everything. She made me look like an unfeeling monster.

MELANIE. You're not a monster.

MIKE *(Overlapping* **MELANIE.***)* I'm not a monster. I did it because…

MELANIE. You love me.

MIKE. *(He stops.)* Yes. Because I love you.

MELANIE. I know that, Mike. I was just so hurt and angry. I couldn't see past the humiliation. I couldn't…I wouldn't see the truth.

MIKE. You know I would never intentionally hurt you.

MELANIE. I know that. It's just that – it's hard to explain, so that you can understand –*(She stands and walks away. Pause.)* It seems like all of my life – at least since I can remember, I've been the heavy girl. My friends were all thinner than me, if by only five or ten pounds, they were thinner. Then after I had Keith, I never lost the weight I gained. I've lived with the pressure of being overweight for more years than I want to admit. But with you – you never seemed to care. I always felt loved by you. Even if I was unhappy with my body, you made me feel like I was beautiful – no matter what.

MIKE. And you are. I just – I knew you were unhappy about it, and I wanted to – I don't know – I just wanted to fix it.

MELANIE. I know. But you can't always fix everything for me, Mike. This can't be fixed unless I make up my mind to do it. And it can't come from you, or *Facing*

Facts, or even a fabulous spa. It has to come from me. I have to figure out how to do this on my own. You know, it's funny.

MIKE. What?

MELANIE. All of this. I love – or rather, I *used* to love *Facing Facts*. I never realized how the people on the show felt until it happened to me. What does that say about me?

MIKE. It's just human nature, Mel. We all do it…like the impulse we get driving by a wreck. We strain our necks around, trying to see what happened. Traffic backs up for miles from rubbernecking.

MELANIE. I guess we've kind of been through a wreck, haven't we? An emotional wreck.

MIKE. Yeah, you could say that. So…how do we put the pieces back together?

MELANIE. I'm not sure. Got a giant bottle of Elmer's glue handy?

MIKE. *(Laughs. Reaches into his pocket.)* No…But I have this little one. *(Pulls out a small bottle of Elmer's.)*

MELANIE. *(Laughing.)* No, you do not! Why in the world…?

MIKE. I broke the handle on the coffee pot. There's no glue at the apartment, so I picked it up when I bought the flowers. Quite a coincidence, huh?

MELANIE. I'd say more like an epiphany.

MIKE. What?

MELANIE. Fate.

MIKE. So what's our fate, Melanie?

MELANIE. I don't know, Mike. There's still so much to work through…I…I just don't know.

MIKE. I do know this, Melanie. I love you – every bit of you. No matter what.

MELANIE. I love you, too, Mike.

MIKE. I want to come home, Melanie.

MELANIE. *(She breaks away.)* Oh, Mike… I –

MIKE. I need to be with you again.

MELANIE. I...I'm just not ready to...to jump right back to where we were. So much has happened.

MIKE. What can we do? We have to start somewhere.

MELANIE. Well...we could start by...by going out for coffee some morning.

MIKE. Melanie...I can't go back to square one.

MELANIE. And I can't go forward unless we do.

MIKE. I see.…Are you sure…?

MELANIE. Yes. I'm sure.

MIKE. Okay...well then –

(He shakes his head and starts towards the door, putting the glue on the dining table as he passes it.)

MELANIE. *(She quickly crosses toward the door.)* How about tomorrow?

MIKE. *(He shakes his head, then stops, relenting.)* I – I guess it'll be...coffee...tomorrow... Well, I'll see you –

MELANIE. Tomorrow.

MIKE. Tomorrow...I'll see you.

*(He reaches for the door handle as **MELANIE** does; their eyes meet.)*

MELANIE. See you.

(He exits. She shuts the door, stares into the room a moment, crosses to flowers, sees the glue, picks it up and realizes her craziness.)

What am I doing?

(She starts for the door, but the phone rings.)

Who would –

(She hurriedly crosses to the phone on coffee table.)

Hello? ...Hi, there...

*(**MIKE** is at the window; he taps it. She turns toward him, laughs, crosses to window, and opens it.)*

MIKE. The thing is, Mel, I never could drink coffee on an

empty stomach.
MELANIE. That's true.
MIKE. So…breakfast?
MELANIE. Breakfast.
MIKE. Where?
MELANIE. How about here?
MIKE. Yeah!

>*(He comes through the window. He tickles and chases her toward the sofa as she laughs and shrieks, they kiss as the lights go out.)*

The End

COSTUME PLOT

ACT I

Scene 1

MELANIE – Light khaki pants, coral t-shirt, light colored, large print, button-up short sleeved shirt, tennis shoes, thin tummy pad to make her look about 15 to 20 pounds heavier, eyeglasses *(The effect is to look at least 30 pounds heavier than in Act II.)*; long-haired wig with bangs

MIKE – Blue jeans, pink pastel polo shirt, slip-on boat shoes; changes to light blue pajama pants, navy cotton robe

PAULA – Black capri pants, black and white small checked shirt, black sandals, reading glasses *(on head.)*

VICTOR – Khaki pants, black button up shirt with tan palm tree design on lower corner, brown and black casual shoes

KEITH – Blue jeans, striped knit polo shirt, t-shirt underneath, brown casual shoes

RICKY – Light brown, white, and khaki plaid pants, light brown t-shirt, slip-on tennis shoes, baseball cap turned backwards, wide-band watch

Scene 2

MELANIE – Light blue pants, light green knit shirt with white lace inlay, tennis shoes, tummy pad, eyeglasses, wig

MIKE – Black jersey work out shorts, baseball shirt – grey body with ¾ black sleeves with Giacobi Construction lettering, red baseball cap, tennis shoes; changes to dark grey suit pants, striped long sleeved shirt, black dress shoes

PAULA – Black capri work out pants with white stripe, light blue knit shirt, tennis shoes, reading glasses *(on head.)*

BOZ – Black jeans, black T-shirt with *Facing Fact*s logo in upper corner, black baseball cap, kneepads, black boots, utility-type belt with candy bars in hoops

MONICA – Black pants, black shirt, black shoes

FRANCES – Tight navy pants suit, with short sleeves, very low cut; big silver dangling earrings and bracelet, high heels

KEITH – Khaki pants, short-sleeved button down white and blue striped shirt, tennis shoes

Scene 3

MIKE – Dark grey suit, loosened tie, blue dress shirt, no under shirt, black dress shoes, black dress watch

MONICA – Black leggings, green, white, black and brown print dress, black wedge shoes, green clutch purse, bangle bracelets, wide-band watch

KEITH – Khaki pants, tan, white, and light blue plaid dress shirt, sleeves rolled up

PAULA – Brown pants, burgundy knit shirt, brown open-toe shoes

VICTOR – Blue jeans, long sleeved denim shirt with Giacobi Construction embroidered over the pocket, brown casual shoes, sports jacket

ACT II

Scene 1

MIKE – Brown dress pants, brown, black, and white striped dress shirt, nice black t-shirt, black dress shoes and socks

KEITH – Blue jeans, light brown, blue and white plaid shirt, nice brown t-shirt, brown casual shoes

PAULA – Burgundy dress, black dress shoes

VICTOR – Khaki pants, Giacobi Construction shirt, brown belt and brown casual shoes

RICKY – Blue jeans, dark brown, red and off-white plaid shirt, light brown t-shirt, slip on tennis shoes

BOZ – Same as Act I

MONICA – Black dress with gold embroidery, black wedge shoes

FRANCES. – Tight black, low-cut halter dress, big gold dangling earrings, big red rhinestone ring, black high heels

MELANIE – Black halter dress with shrug that ties in front, black strappy high heels, rhinestone earrings, no tummy pad

Scene 2

MIKE – Blue jeans, nice black t-shirt from previous scene, casual black slip on shoes

KEITH – Nice brown t-shirt from previous scene, brown, white, and teal plaid shorts, tennis shoes, short white socks

Scene 3

MELANIE – Black pants, flattering small muted print purple and black blouse with black lace accent, casual black shoes, hoop earrings; changes shirt to flattering black and pink blouse, dressy black shoes

PAULA – Black capri pants, black t-shirt with small multi-colored dots, black sandals

KEITH – Blue jeans, blue, black and white stripped shirt, nice black shoes

MONICA – Burgundy halter-top, white, burgundy, and rose print skirt, beige wedges, chunky necklace, purse

Scene 4

RICKY – Kelly green gym shorts, argyle socks, bandana tied around head, navy t-shirt with 'Six Pack Abs' and the top of a six-pack of beer printed on it, slip on tennis shoes

KEITH – Grey jersey workout shorts, royal blue jersey shirt, tennis shoes, short socks

PAULA – Navy capri pants, wedgewood blue blouse, navy casual shoes

MELANIE – Black pants, flattering shirt with small print in blues, black and white, black casual shoes

VICTOR – Light blue jeans, subdued Hawaiian print shirt, gold chain, sandals, white socks

Scene 5

MELANIE – Black pants with slits ten inches up the side, dressy red and black blouse, dressy black sandals

MIKE – Dark grey suit pants, long sleeved grey, white, and blue striped shirt, black dress shoes

PROPERTY AND FURNITURE PLOT

Furniture and walls
Round dining table with four chairs
Tablecloth
Hutch
Casual chandelier over table
Small wine table DR of kitchen door with several bottles of wine in rack, at least two open holes, books on top of wine table
Long sofa
Coffee table
Large rug under coffee table, extended down stage about three feet from table
Chair
Drop leaf table near arch with pictures and note pad holder
Family pictures on wall over drop leaf table
Floor lamp by drop leaf table
Decorative items on tables and hutch, flower arrangements, pictures, etc. *(very little on coffee table.)*
Decorative pictures on walls
Three way light switch by front door
Two way light switch by arch
Family pictures on hall wall
Sheers and window scarf on window
Wooden porch railing
Painted neighborhood mural on back wall
Ferns hanging behind window on back wall

Props
Act I, Scene 1

Pre-set
Window open, sheers closed

On round dining table
Card deck on table at Melanie's chair
Wine glasses on table at women's chairs
Beer bottles on table at men's chairs
Note pad and pencil on table at Victor's chair
Bowl with small amount of crackers on table

On hutch
Five or six board games, one being Catch Phrase
Case for deck of cards

On sofa
Four pillows and Afghan throw

On coffee table
Photography book
Remote control for television

Hand props
Wine glass with white wine, beer bottle – Mike
Wine glass with red wine, beer bottle – Paula
Empty tray – Melanie
Box of Ding Dongs, Little Debbie Nutty Butty Bars, Little Debbie oatmeal cookie pies, two boxes of crackers, plate of little sausages, two water bottles, unopened bag of pretzels – Keith and Ricky
Tissue – Paula
Dropped cracker – Ricky
Glass of water – Keith
Kitchen towel – Keith

Act I, Scene 2

Pre-set
Window closed, sheers closed
Remote control hidden behind a sofa pillow
Note pad and pencil have been moved back to drop leaf table

Hand props
Covered bowl of dip, duffle bag, reading glasses – Paula
Tray with crackers, drinks – Melanie
Baseball glove – Mike
Chocolate pinwheel cookie bag, open; one cookie out – Melanie
Television camera with microphone and light attached – Boz
Microphone – Frances
Make-up bag, small bag or cooler for water bottles, towel – Monica
Melanie's suitcase – Mike

Act I, Scene 3

Pre-set
Window closed, sheers open
TV remote control on coffee table
Monica's clutch purse on floor beside sofa

Hand props
Keys, mail – Mike
Cell phone, lip gloss *(in purse.)* – Monica
Big covered roasting pot – Paula
Bag of pretzels *(unopened.)*, bottle of beer – Mike

Act II, Scene 1

Pre-set
Window closed, sheers closed

On round dining table
Bowl of crackers, bowl of chips

Bowl with whipped cream *(as dip.)*
Napkins
Wet-one folded like a napkin
TV remote control on coffee table

Hand props
Boz – same as Act I
Monica – same as Act I
Frances – same as Act I
Mike's suitcase – Melanie

Act II, Scene 2

Window closed, sheers closed
Fashion magazine, People type magazine on coffee table

Hand props
Cell phone – Keith

Act II, Scene 3

Window closed, sheers closed
Fashion magazine, *People* type magazine on coffee table

Hand Props
Several shopping bags, one from Soma lingerie with red push-up bra covered with tissue paper, purse, front door keys – Melanie
Two blouses with tags in a shopping bag – Melanie
Cordless phone, yellow pages – Melanie
Purse – Monica

Act II, Scene 4

Preset
Window closed, sheers closed
Note pad and pencil on drop leaf table *(previously set.)*

Hand Props
Tennis racket in bag – Ricky
Tennis racket – Keith
Four full plastic grocery bags *(one of which is Melanie's.)* – Paula
Four full plastic grocery bags, purse – Melanie
Cordless phone – Melanie

Act II, Scene 5

Preset
Window closed, sheers opened
Melanie's purse on table with compact inside

Hand Props
Roses in tissue paper – Mike
Vase – Melanie
Smallest bottle of Elmer's glue – Mike

The Makeover was written with each specific character's thoughts and feelings in mind. The dialogue is appropriate to the characters and their feelings within the context. However, if it is necessary to delete certain words, the following dialogue may be substituted:

Act I, Scene 1
Pg. 10 Victor: Quit your bitchin'! (Quit your whinin'!)
Pg. 10 Paula: The bitcher… (The whiner…)
Pg. 11 Victor: What the hell is wrong with girls? (What's wrong with girls?)
Pg. Paula: Oh my god! (Oh my goodness!)
Pg. 11 Victor: Will you play your damn card, woman! (Cut damn.)
Pg. 11 Victor: I don't see how you can stand that damn show. (…that stupid show.)
Pg. 11 Victor: It's just a bunch of rigged crap. (…rigged bunk.)
Pg. 12 Victor: That's bullshit. (That's bull!)
Pg. 13 Victor: Oh for chrissakes… (Oh, for Pete's sake…)
Pg. 13 Victor: Holy crap! I'd come out of there with gelled hair… (You gotta be kiddin'! I'd come out…)
Pg. 14 Victor: You got me so damn flustered… (Use darn or cut damn.)
Pg. 15 Victor: You have that female intuition crap… (Stop at intuition.)
Pg. 17 Victor: I don't remember what was so damn funny… (Use darn.)
Pg. 23 Ricky: …screwing around like that… (Use messing.)
Pg. 24 Keith: Oh my god! (Oh, no!)
Pg. 24 Ricky: More like goddess. (Oh, yes!)
Pg. 24 Keith: Oh my god! You've been doing our Western Lit teacher… (No way! You've been…)
Pg. 25 Keith: Oh my god! She is hot! (Cut Oh my god.)
Pg. 25 Ricky: …come from 'Mary Jane'… (stuffs Ding Dong in mouth) Oh my god. (Cut Oh my god.)
Pg. 26 Ricky: It's not like that, ass wipe. (It's not like that, jerk.)
Pg. 26 Ricky: Hell, no! (No way!)… He'd kick my ass (He'd kick my butt.)
Pg. 27 Ricky: Bullshit, Mom. (That's bull, Mom.)
Pg. 28 Ricky: Oh my god! {when he sees cracker on the floor.} (Oh!)

Act I, Scene 2
Pg. 31 Melanie: My god! She is vicious… (Wow! She is…)
Pg. 32 Paula: Damn it! Now she's going to miss… (Shoot! Now she's going…)
Pg. 37 Frances: Damn it! Here! (Oh! Or just a grunt. Here!)
Pg. 38 Frances: Thank God! That was a tough one… (Finally! That was a…)

Act I, Scene 3
Pg. 43 Monica: Oh my god! I would totally die. (Oh, no! I would…)
Pg. 44 Monica: …should rot in hell for what she did… (…should rot in hades…)
Pg. 48 Victor: I know what the damn word means. (I know what the word means.)

Pg. 49 Victor: I can't do a damn thing right. (I can't do anything right!)
Pg. 50 Paula: …Sometimes you irritate the hell out of me, Victor! (Sometimes you irritate me to death, Victor!)
Pg. 51 Mike: …it's going to stay that way, you bastard! (Cut you bastard.)

Act II, Scene 1
Pg. 52 Mike: Oh my god! I think I'm going to have a coronary. (Oh! Or grunt. I think…)
Pg. 52 Ricky: … work with that bitch. (…work with that witch.)
Pg. 53 Victor: Watch your damn mouth, Ricky. (Cut damn.) Add: Ricky. What? I said witch! Victor. Oh. Okay, then. Then Mike yells 'Quiet. It's on.'
Pg. 53 Mike: …banshee from hell. (Cut from hell.)
Pg. 53 Mike: Oh my god! They're here. (Cut Oh my god!)
Pg. 55 Keith: Oh my god! She… (Cut Oh My god. Use She what-?)
Pg. 62 Boz: Hell, you made my year. (In fact, you made my year.)

Act II, Scene 3
Pg. 70 Keith: Oh my god! (Oh, no!)

Act II, Scene 4
Pg. 74 Keith: Oh my god! You and my mom! (Cut Oh my god! Use What?!)
Pg. 74 Keith: Where the hell did you learn that? (Where did you learn to do that!?)
Pg. 76 Melanie: I'm… I'm such a bitch. (I'm… I'm such a witch.)
Pg. 78 Victor: You are looking so damn good since… (Cut damn.)
Pg. 80 Melanie: …I'm not going to put up with your crap anymore. (I'm not going to put up with it any more.)
Pg. 80 Melanie: God, I feel sorry for Paula. (I feel so sorry for Paula.)
Pg. 80 Victor: Why the hell would I do that? (Why the heck would I do that?)
Pg. 81 Paula: …I have put up with your crap for over… (I have put up with you for over…)
Pg. 81 Victor: …and I don't need a damn shrink. (Cut damn.)
Pg. 81 Victor: Who the hell are you to tell me… (Cut the hell.)

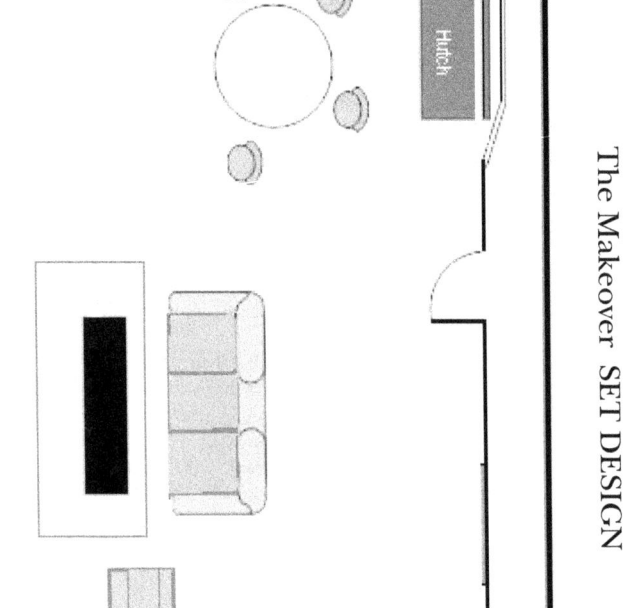

The Makeover SET DESIGN

From the Reviews of
THE MAKEOVER...

"The new comedy-drama *The Makeover* is satisfying ... and highly pleasurable... Daussat's play is quite entertaining and she earns a solid, robust share of laughs from her writing. (She) has a keen sense of humor... Issues of being overweight in this country are presented ... with brutal honesty, never once sounding preachy or whining, but instead with a truthful, immensely heartfelt observation... Daussat's talents are shown to be off to a great start... a solid audience pleaser... a knockout hit."
- John Garcia, *Talkin' Broadway*

"Daussat knows the basics of writing a situational script: She sets up the characters and action nicely, and gives the characters interesting quirks and vibrant lines to speak... (The) message about learning to love yourself (is) peppered with ... comedy (and is) heartfelt... *The Makeover* should become a popular title in theaters..."
- Mark Lowry, *Fort Worth Star Telegram*

OTHER TITLES AVAILABLE FROM SAMUEL FRENCH

ELECTION DAY
Josh Tobiessen

Full Length / Comedy / 2m, 2f / Unit Set

It's Election Day, and Adam knows his over-zealous girlfriend will never forgive him if he fails to vote. But when his sex starved sister, an eco-terrorist, and a mayoral candidate willing to do anything for a vote all show up, Adam finds that making that quick trip to the polls might be harder than he thought. *Election Day* is a hilarious dark comedy about the price of political (and personal) campaigns.

"An outrageous comedy… at double-espresso speed."
- *The New York Times*

"Ridiculously entertaining… cute and cutting."
- *Variety*

"Laugh-out-loud."
- *Backstage*

"Delightfully farcical… Tobiessen takes a simple premise and spins it out into a hilarious sequence of events. His dialogue is lean and playful, and includes some terrific lines."
- *Theatermania*

SAMUELFRENCH.COM

OTHER TITLES AVAILABLE FROM SAMUEL FRENCH

A VERY MERRY UNAUTHORIZED CHILDREN'S SCIENTOLOGY PAGEANT
Kyle Jarrow

Musical / 5m, 5f (Doubling possible) / Interior

A jubilant cast of children celebrate the controversial religion in uplifting pageantry and song. The actual teachings of The Church of Scientology are explained and dissected against the candy-colored backdrop of a traditional nativity play. Pageant is a musical biography of the life of L. Ron Hubbard, with child-friendly explanations of Hubbard's notion of the divided mind (embodied by the lovely identical twins Emma and Sophie Whitfield in matching brain outfits) and a device called the e-meter (or electropsychometer), used to monitor the human psyche, which is demonstrated by stick puppets. Grade school children, portraying Tom Cruise, Kirstie Alley, John Travolta, and other less starry Scientologists, brings the controversial Church of Scientology to jubilant life in story and song.

SAMUELFRENCH.COM

www.ingramcontent.com/pod-product-compliance
Lightning Source LLC
Chambersburg PA
CBHW050514020526
44111CB00052B/2282